FIRM FOUNDATION

Christian Discipleship Manual

Reverend Wayne E. A. Palmer

2018

FIRM FOUNDATION – CHRISTIAN DISCIPLESHIP MANUAL

ISBN: 978-976-96123-5-8

Published by: The Publisher's Notebook Limited
email: PUBLISHER@thepublishersnotebook.com

THE PUBLISHER'S NOTEBOOK LIMITED
PUBLISHERS FOR THE CHRISTIAN GENRE

DEDICATION

The question was asked of me "to whom are you dedicating this book?" My initial thought was "wow, a dedication, what exactly is that?" My next response was to commit it to prayer and then it made perfect sense. I was being given an opportunity to say thanks to some unsung hero, a name that when mentioned would not immediately set off any bell of recognition. However, their names are known before the throne of His Majesty on High, JESUS, and their labor was not in vain. I therefore dedicate this book to the following persons in honor of the contributions they made in my life in area of discipleship.

- ✓ My blood brother Mr. Ruben Palmer. Growing up as a child I looked up to him because of his unshakeable love for the Lord and the things of the Lord, how as a young man he modeled faithfulness even to this very day. He made me wanted to love the Lord just the same way. To me he is discipleship by example. I love you my brother.
- ✓ Mr. Noel Knight. His knowledge of the Word and method of imparting that Word has help to shape the passion and love I have the Holy Scripture. I can still hear in my spirit his teachings on sanctification and justification they were liberating. His was discipleship by the impartation of truth, a byproduct of rightly dividing the Holy Scriptures.
- ✓ Mr. Patrick Brunette, Mr. Steve Yee Sing (now home with the Lord) Mr. Orville Warren and Mr. Christopher Beckford. These men help to chisel my life with the truth of Scripture. They have mastered the art of discipleship

through small group gatherings, mentorship and clean healthy interactions and peer to peer accountability.

✓ And last but not least the late Rev. Cedrick Lue. For his passion and love for youth, and his ability to spot the greatness in you take steps to father and develop that seed into a mighty tree. He provided pastoral discipleship with heart of David.

My hope is that this manual will be an inspiration to anyone that is serious about fulfilling Matthew 28:19, 20. To go, to teach: - disciple all nations, to baptize and to teaching: -producing a believer/ follower that will observe: - to keep their eyes upon the things which the Lord commands even to His return.

Rev. Wayne E. A. Palmer

Table of Contents

Foreword – Apostle Dr Steve & Pastor Dr Michelle Lyston v

Foreword – Jim & Dawn Munroe vi

Preface vii

Acknowledgements x

Introduction xi

How To Receive Christ And Have Assurance Of Salvation 1

Acknowledge 1

Recognize that God's plan for man is life and peace 1

What did Jesus do? 2

How do I experience God's provision? 2

Experiencing the assurance of salvation 2

The Truth And Power Of Water Baptism 4

What is Water Baptism? 4

Reasons we should be water baptized 5

What Name should we be baptized in? 5

How to be assured that we have been baptized into Jesus Christ
.... 7

The Scriptural Way To Deal With Temptation, Sin And Guilt 9

What is temptation and how are we tempted? 10

What is sin, how can we overcome it? 10

The effects of sin on mankind 11

How to Experience Forgiveness of Sins 12

Deliverance from Deonic Influence 13

    Demonic Practices Forbidden 14

    Definition of selected words (Deuteronomy 18: 9 - 14)............ 15

    Steps to receiving and keeping your deliverance 17

Empowered by The Holy Spirit 19

    His purpose for coming 21

    Examples of His activities in the Scriptures............................. 22

    Some phrases used to describe Him in the Old Testament 22

    His work in the Believer's life.. 22

    The Baptism of the Holy Spirit 23

    The Holy Spirit's effect on our lives (The Gifts and Fruit)........... 24

Growing in Our Relationship with God 26

    God's Attitude towards a Christian's Prayer 26

    Growing through studying the Word 27

    The benefits of studying and applying/living the scriptures 28

    How to have an effective personal Bible study 29

    How to make The Bible come alive 30

    The Basic Rules That Govern The Interpretation Of The Bible... 30

Growing through Thanksgiving, Praise, and Worship 34

    How we should praise and thank the Lord 34

    The ascending levels of Praise 35

    Why do we Praise and Thank the Lord................................ 44

    Examples of Praise and Thanksgiving and the results 45

Positions or Postures in Worship.................................. 46

Results of spending time waiting on or worshiping God............ 46

Relationship Names of God (Hebrew Names) 47

The Burden of Stewardship.................................. 49

Stewardship over spiritual things 49

Stewardship over material things................................ 50

Stewardship over first fruits and offerings...................... 50

What is the first fruit? 51

Stewardship over the tithes..................................... 52

Other scriptures on the principle of stewardship/giving 53

Mindsets that must be overcome as steward 53

Growing through Obedience.................................. 54

Obedience defined 54

Results of obedience 55

Fellowship with the Saints.................................. 56

Unity must be our watchword.................................... *56*

The Future Fate of Mankind 59

Future fate of the Righteous.................................... 60

Future fate of the wicked....................................... 60

The Ministry of Reconciliation 62

The basic gospel message 62

Penalties of sin.. 63

Jesus – The sacrifice that paid the price for sin 63

How to Reconcile a Person to God 64

What happens to the person that accepts Jesus as Lord? 64

What does Jesus expect from us as Believers? 65

Sharing The Gospel (your faith) 65

An example to remember 66

How can we be born again? 67

Just how did Jesus make this provision? 67

How do we make use of this provision? 67

God's Standard of Morality 70

Homosexuality /Sodomy 71

Adultery and fornication 78

Incest 79

Biblical Morality and Church Leadership 82

Preventative Guidelines 83

Curative Guidelines 84

Examples of God judgment on Irresponsible leadership 87

Old Testament laws that Eli should have observed to deal with the sins of his sons 91

A word of advice 91

The Biblically Required Response From Leadership 92

Victim Support/Help 93

Brawta 95

About the Author 97

Foreword – Apostle Dr Steve & Pastor Dr Michelle Lyston

Having read this book, we both agree that this is a powerful tool for anyone who wants to understand the very basic tenets and requirements of being a disciple of Jesus Christ. It gives pertinent information with clarity, and that is particularly vital today in light of all the information flooding our lives daily. It is an easy read because it is written in clear, basic and concise language. It is absolutely full of great information that is pertinent to the life of every individual who desires to serve the Lord in Spirit and in Truth.

This book is timely and has the potential to unlock a better understanding not only of Discipleship, but also of the importance of a true and strong relationship with God and of knowing what He requires of us. This is quite a helpful book and a powerful tool to have in your arsenal.

Apostle Dr. Steve & Pastor Dr. Michelle Lyston
Authors - Tactics and Strategies for the Famine: & In His Presence: Maintaining the Presence of God Through Worship
Restoration World Outreach Ministries Inc

Foreword – Jim & Dawn Munroe

Firm Foundation is a must have and a must read for new and mature believers alike. This powerful, yet practical discipleship manual is built on a solid uncompromising Biblical foundation which anchors the believer from spiritual infancy to intimacy with Jesus Christ. In this book, Apostle Wayne inspires the readers to constantly reflect on their own stance and position in Jesus Christ. His anointed, contextualized teaching makes this a relevant and vital tool in an unsettled spiritual world. If we understand and live by the anointed coaching this manual provides, we can experience great victory against the subtle and direct attacks of the enemy of our souls.

I encourage each person who reads this book to read it prayerfully and with great expectation.

Jim & Dawn Munroe
Deacon, Counseling Psychologist
Jubilee Worship Center

Preface

This book came about after years of ministering to and preparing thousands of new believers across denominational lines for a deeper, Scripture-led, scripture-anchored, 'Christ as cornerstone' life. In one of the churches I served as an assistant pastor, discipleship and church growth was part of my job description. Those fresh and hungry, for the knowledge of God's heart and mind, would ask questions as they were now discovering that not many were happy that they were now saved and serving the Lord. They also encountered those that would attempt to shipwreck their faith with complex, biblical argument and questions. Another challenge they faced, was that of being saved and living in what was called "the real world."

Out of my deep love for the Lord and His people, I would do hours, months and years of research in the scripture as well as take notes of every preacher that came to us (such as Rev. Seaton D. Wilson) to establish an accurate, biblical foundation for what they were teaching. These new believers were eager to know God, His Word, and His Way. I would also collect well-researched teachings from other speakers and get their full permission to modify where necessary to give a more fulsome picture of the biblical subject under consideration. One such speaker was Pastor David Ferguson.

The greatest portions were birthed out of my own private time with YHVH and Him instructing me on what areas to cover and how to approach each topic. Needless to say, this book has been finished several times and was even sent to be published by another publisher, but it would not go through I had to take it back and add more information to deliver a more fulsome picture of the mind of Christ on each subject matter covered herein. I can hear the injunctions from the Apostle Paul shout back at me as he said to Timothy and Titus,

"If you put these things before the brothers, you will be a good servant of Christ Jesus, being trained in the words of the faith and of the good doctrine that you have followed." (Timothy 4:6)ESV. And again,

"If anyone teaches a different doctrine and does not agree with the sound words of our Lord Jesus Christ and the teaching that accords with godliness, he is puffed up with conceit and understands nothing. He has an unhealthy craving for controversy and for quarrels about words, which produce envy, dissension, slander, evil suspicions, and constant friction among people who are depraved in mind and deprived of the truth, imagining that godliness is a means of gain".(Timothy 6:3-5) ESV. And yet again,

"Show yourself in all respects to be a model of good works, and in your teaching show integrity, dignity, and sound speech that cannot be condemned, so that an opponent may be put to shame, having nothing evil to say about us." (Titus 2:7, 8)ESV. And finally, "I charge you in the presence of God and of Christ Jesus, who is to judge the living and the dead, and by his appearing and his kingdom: preach the word; be ready in season and out of season; reprove, rebuke, and exhort, with complete patience and teaching. For the time is coming when people will not endure sound teaching, but having itching ears, they will accumulate for themselves teachers to suit their own passions and will turn away from listening to the truth and wander off into myths." (2 Timothy 4:1-4)ESV.

This is my life's mandate. "… and what you have heard from me in the presence of many witnesses entrust to faithful men, who will be able to teach others also…" (2 Timothy 2:2) ESV.

Acknowledgements

It has been said that a great partnership causes small businesses to become great big organizations. With this in mind, I wish to say thank you to the following persons: first to "The Lord Jesus our Lord, the King of Glory" for the insight, wisdom and the spiritual foundation necessary to complete this book.

Thanks to my wife and sons for their willingness to share my personal and family time that should have been spent on them, on this book. Exceptional thanks to Melody, my wife, for your encouragement, push, and your dedication to proofread this book for its speedy completion. Thank you, Patricka (Pat) Graham for your work up front, as well as behind the scenes, making links, contacts and researching publishers and printers. Thank you, Tricia Shay Gray, for coming on board with your expertise and professional insight on the original formatting as well as designing the first cover for the book. I also extend thanks to Jubilee Worship Centre, Mrs. Sandra Gallimore and Lue Bell and the many others for your prayers, thoughts, well wishes and financial gifts to make this book possible.

Thank you to The Publisher's Notebook Ltd, and you Team for taking on this challenge and for making publishing this first project a reality. May the Lord make your gift, input and support resound back to you and your house as a great blessing breaking debt and establishing a generational blessing with great prosperity?

Introduction

The purpose of this discipleship manual is to equip those who have come to faith through the saving knowledge of Jesus Christ and His redeeming sacrifice on the cross. I hope that it will truly empower each person to be an active "living stone" (member) of the Body of Christ, doing his/her part in the advancement of His kingdom.

This manual rises above the spirit of denominationalism by making the teaching of the Bible simple enough to be milk to the babies in Christ, yet bread and meat enough, even for those who have come of age. It is presented in a format that defines and points us to the Word of God, and where each teaching can be found. I, therefore, put the name of the Lord upon you in this Aaronic blessing.

"YHVH / The LORD bless you and keep you; the LORD make his face to shine upon you and be gracious to you; YHVH / The LORD lift up His countenance upon you and give you peace. So shall they put my name upon the people of Israel, and I will bless them." Amen. (Numbers 6:24-27) ESV.

Reverend Wayne E. A. Palmer

FIRM FOUNDATION

Christian Discipleship Manual

1

How To Receive Christ And Have Assurance Of Salvation

Acknowledge

All men outside of a relationship with Jesus Christ are sinners and as such are under God's judgment

(i) All men have sinned against God (Romans 3: 23)

(ii) Unregenerate man is not in right standing with God (Romans 3: 10 – 12)

(iii) God has concluded all men to be under sin – (Galatians 3: 22.)

(iv) God's judgment for sin is death – (Romans 6: 23a.)

(v) The final judgment for all sinners is the lake of fire which is called the Second death – (Revelations 21: 8)

(vi) Those that misuse kingdom resources will go into everlasting punishment - (Matthew 25:46)

Recognize that God's plan for man is life and peace.

(i) Jesus came to give us abundant life – (John 10: 10.)

(ii) Eternal life is the gift of God – (Romans 6: 23b.)

(iii) Jesus promised rest and peace to those who come to Him – (Matthew 11: 28)

What did Jesus do?

(i) Jesus died for us – (Romans 5: 8.)
(ii) Jesus is the only person God has provided through whom we can come into a relationship with Him – (John 14: 6; Acts 4: 12)

How do I experience God's provision?

(i) He gives eternal life to those that believe in Him (John 3:16)
(ii) Those who receive (accept) Jesus into their heart will be given the right/privilege to be called the sons (children) of God – (John 1: 12.)
(iii) If we believe that God raised Jesus from the dead, we are declared to be righteous, and if we confess Him as our Lord, we shall be saved– (Romans 10: 9 – 10.)
(iv) We also need to repent (turn) and believe the Gospel – (Mark 1: 15.)

Experiencing the assurance of salvation

We need to be aware of this teaching/doctrine as is taught in the Scriptures:

(i) Those who receive Christ become sons of God – (John 1: 12 – 13.)
(ii) Those who believe that Jesus is the Christ are born of God – (1 John 5: 1.)
(iii) Three things happen to the person who hears the words of Jesus Christ and believes in Him who sent him. (a) He has everlasting life, (b) He shall not come into condemnation, and (c) he passes from death into life – John 5: 24.
(iv) God has given us eternal life (eternal in quality as well as quantity), and this life is found in His Son Jesus Christ – 1John 5: 11 – 12.

(v) The things that were written in the first epistle of John were done so that we who believe on the name of Jesus would know that we have eternal life– (1 John 5:13.)

(vi) Jesus went to prepare a place for us, and when He comes back He will receive us to Himself so that we will always live wherever He lives– (John 14: 2 – 3.)

(vii) When we come to Jesus, He has promised that He will never cast us out nor turn us away – (John 6: 37.)

(viii) No man is able to pluck us out of Jesus' hands – (John 10: 27 - 28.)

(ix) Jesus delivers us from the wrath/judgment to come – (1 Thessalonians 1: 10.)

(x) The Father will honor us because we serve Christ – (John 12: 26.)

(xi) We who believe in Jesus will be raised up on the last day – (John 6: 40.)

(xii) He has given us his divine nature and all that we need to live Godly in these present times. (2 Peter 1:3-12)

2

The Truth And Power Of Water Baptism

What is Water Baptism?

> _"He that believeth and is baptized shall be saved: but he that believeth not shall be damned."– (Mark 16:16)_

We are instructed by the Scriptures to be baptized in water, but what is water baptism and what are the reasons that the Scriptures give for us doing it? The word baptism is taken from the Greek word _"baptizo"_ which has its root in the word _"bapto"_. _"Baptizo"_ means to immerse, submerge, plunge and overwhelm, while _"bapto"_ means to dip. Baptism, therefore, means to immerse a person in water.

This point of immersing a person during the act of baptism is borne out by the following examples: - Jesus' baptism – (Matthew 3:16) "And Jesus, when he was baptized, _went up straightway out of the water...";_ and the Ethiopian eunuch – (Acts 8:38 – 39) "And he commanded the chariot to stand still, and _they went down both into the water,_ both Phillip, and the eunuch; and he baptized him. And when _they were come up out of the water,_ the Spirit of the Lord caught away Phillip..." As you can see in both examples ",

4

they came up out of," suggesting that they had previously gone down into the water.

Reasons we should be water baptized

Listed below are some of the reasons that the Scriptures give why we should be water baptized.

(i)   It is a command from God to all Believers. (Matthew 28:19)
(ii) It is the "act of burial" in our identification with the death, burial and the bodily resurrection of our Lord Jesus. (Romans 6:1-11.) This physical act spiritually buries the old man who is now dead.
(iii) By faith we experience the same deliverance that the children of Israel experienced at the crossing of the Red Sea – (Exodus 14:22-30, 1 Corinthians10:1-2.) Pharaoh (a type of Satan) and his army were cut off from recapturing the children of Israel (the Believer). We can choose to return to him, but he can't cross over to us.
(iv) We are following the example of Jesus – (Matthew 3:13-17.)
(v)   Baptism symbolizes the washing away of sins – (Acts 22:16.)
(vi) It was a foundational doctrine of the early church – (Acts 2:41, Acts 10:47-48.) It is seen as a form of spiritual circumcision – (Colossians 2:11-12.)

What Name should we be baptized in?

There has been a controversy about the formula used in water baptism. Some say that it should be done in the name of the Father, Son and the Holy Spirit (this is based on Matthew 28:19) and some say that it should be done in the name of Jesus (based on Acts 2:38 and other references in the New Testament).

(i)   In all the references in the book of Acts where Believers were baptized, and a name was mentioned, it was the name of **Jesus** the Christ – (Acts 2:38; 8:16; 10:48 and 19:5.)

(ii) In Matthew 28:19 the phrase is used "the name" not "the names." The singular "name" suggests one name to which the Godhead responds; the Father will respond to prayers prayed in Jesus' name, the Son is Jesus, and the Holy Spirit came in the name of Jesus.

(iii) We are instructed to do everything in the name of the Lord Jesus– (Colossians 3:17.)

(iv) In the act of water baptism, we identify with the death, burial and bodily resurrection of Jesus, not the Father or the Holy Spirit.

A few other things should also be made clear: (a) the formula that is recited over the head of the new Believer upon his/her baptism does not totally confirm or guarantee that the person is truly in Jesus Christ. For example, there were and are cult and occult groups then and now, that used both formulas when baptizing their new converts/initiate (1 John 2:19). John the Baptist said in Matthew 3:7-8 that for one to be baptized, he/she needed to show what John called "meat or fruit" of repentance. In other words, one must demonstrate evidence of actual *conversion* and *submission* to the Lordship of Jesus. The need for this evidence is locked into the phrase "In the name of" which precedes both of the formulas used.

The word "name" (onoma, Greek) used in Matthew 28:19 and all through the book Acts, means **"The authority and character of."** We can now see why no one knows what was recited over the head of Jesus and the countless others who John baptized in Jordan (Mark 1:4-5). Neither does anyone know what formula was recited over the heads of the 2.5 million people baptized all at once as they crossed the Red Sea (1 Corinthians10:2.) certainly been baptized onto Moses does not me "in the name of Moses. "

It is also important to note, that contrary to what some persons teach on the subject, not all the individuals who were baptized by John the Baptist had to be re-baptized using the formula **"in Jesus' name."** (And yes, there were some as in Acts 19:1-7.) However, in Mark 1:4-5: we see where all Judaea came out and was baptized by John the Baptist /Baptizer. Andrew, John's disciple who followed Jesus, was never re-baptized - John 1:36-40. In the Book of Acts, Matthias the replacement Apostle that was baptized by John, but he too was never re-baptized. (Acts 1:21-26.) Finally, we should also remember that no evidence is found anywhere in the book of Acts that shows any of the Twelve Disciples/Apostles were asked to be re-baptized. Using the Formula "In The Name Of Jesus" or even in "The Name of the Father Son and Holy Ghost," even after several outpourings of the Holy Spirit in the book of Acts.

How to be assured that we have been baptized into Jesus Christ

(i)   Our baptism is a testimony of our death to sin (Romans 6:1-3)
(ii) Make no provision for the flesh, by putting on (clothe or array yourself in or with the nature of) the Lord Jesus Christ (Romans 13:12 -14)
(iii) For as many as having been baptized into Christ have put on Christ (Galatians 3:27)
(iv) Baptism saves (deliver or protect) us in the same way Noah and his family were saved (preserve, rescue) in the ark from the flood. (1 Peter 3:20,221)
(v)   This is not the mere putting away of the filth (dirt) of the flesh (body), but (to the contrary) it is the answer (inquiry) of a good conscience (moral consciousness) toward God, by the channel of an act - through the resurrection of Jesus Christ. (1Peter 3:21)
(vi) Anyone who fears God and works righteousness is accepted by God. (Acts 10:34-39)

The use of either of the two formulas then, is one and the same, since there is only one way through which we can be qualify for heaven, and it is to receive Jesus Christ as Lord and Savior, turning away from our sins and maintaining a personal relationship with Jesus the Christ. There is no other name/provision made under heaven by which man can be saved (Acts 4:12; Ephesians 2:8, 9; Philippians 2:10).

There are some who are contentious and ignorantly divide the Body of Christ on such issues. It is not our intention to do so but to be as scripturally correct as possible.

3

The Scriptural Way

To Deal With Temptation,

Sin And Guilt

"For by grace are ye saved through faith, and that not of yourselves, it is the gift of God not of works, lest any man should boast."– (Ephesians 2: 8 – 9)

There hath no temptation taken you but such as is common to man: but God is faithful, who will not suffer you to be tempted above that ye are able; but will with the temptation also make a way to escape, that ye may be able to bear it. – (1 Corinthians 10:13)

"Therefore, if any man be in Christ, he is a new creature, old things are passed away; behold all things are become new."– (2 Corinthians 5: 17)

What is temptation and how are we tempted?

When we are tempted, we are enticed or incited to do a wrong or forbidden thing –Oxford Dictionary. There are also two main characteristic or factors of which a temptation is made, they are the push and the pull factors, and these are somehow rooted in pride. A man is tempted when he is drawn away of **his own** lusts /desires (the push or drive factor) – (James 1:14.) The Bible says of Jesus, "The prince of the world has nothing in common with Jesus, there is nothing in Jesus that belongs to him, and he has no power over Jesus" (John 14:30 Amp.)

Let us examine the first example of sin in the Garden of Eden. God placed man and woman in the Garden Eden to till and guard it; He also placed two trees in the midst of the garden, the tree of life and the tree of the knowledge of good and evil (Genesis 2:9).

When Satan questioned Eve, however, she only saw one tree, the tree of the knowledge of good and evil, which appealed to her very much (the pull, entice or seduction factor) (Genesis 3:1 – 6). It would seem that before Satan brought up the matter she had already thought of it, but it was Satan's question that insight/ignite a desire in her for the tree fruit, The Bible encourages us to abstain (hold oneself off) from all appearance of evil – (1 Thessalonians 5:22-24.) The Bible also says we should do the following; "We destroy arguments and every lofty opinion raised against the knowledge of God, and take every thought captive to obey Christ," (2 Corinthians 10:5) ESV.

What is sin, how can we overcome it?

(i) The Bible says, "Sin is the transgression of the law." – (1 John 3:4.) Another definition of sin is to "miss the mark/target."

(ii) There is a difference between our thoughts and the intents of our hearts – (Hebrews 4:12.)

(iii) Sin is the decision or intent to commit, as well as the act, of wrongdoing – (Matthew 5:28.)

(iv) As Christians we do not have to sin, we have a choice – (1 John 2:1 and Romans 6:12.)

Note, however, that there are three main categories into which all the temptations and all the sins in the world falls. These are the lust of the flesh, the lust of the eyes and the pride of life. (Genesis 3:1-6; Luke 4: 3-13; 1 John 2:15 -17.)

The effects of sin on mankind

The very moment Adam and Eve sinned they, for the first time, felt shame and covered themselves. They also hid themselves, from the Presence of the Lord God – (Genesis 3:7 – 8; Compare Genesis 2:25).

It is important for us to remember that because of the sin of Adam and Eve all human beings were born in sin (Romans 3:23). As a result of this is why we needed a Savior, (Isaiah 53: 6; 1 Peter 2:24, 25.)

When David kept silence about his sin, he experienced physical as well as emotional torment – Psalm 32:3 – 4. Psalm 68: 6 says, "...but the rebellious dwell in a dry land." And in Isaiah 57:20 – 21- "But the wicked are like the troubled sea when it cannot rest, whose waters cast up mire and dirt. There is no peace, saith, my God, to the wicked." KJV.

How to Experience Forgiveness of Sins

(i) We must "own up to" or acknowledge our sins – (Daniel 9:5; Psalms 51:3;1 John 1:9)

(ii) When David acknowledged his sin, he owned it (accepted responsibility). (Psalm 51)

(iii) We must confess our sins. To verbally admit one's guilt to the particular infraction/ transgression (Daniel 9:3-7.) We see the example of King David confessed his sins (Psalms 51:1-19; and the warning of Proverbs 28: 13 "Whoever conceals his transgressions will not prosper, but he who confesses and forsakes them will obtain mercy.") ESV.

(iv) We must turn away from or forsake our sins (Proverbs 28:13; Isaiah 55;7, 2 Chronicles 7:14)

(v) We must ask for forgiveness for our sins (1John 1:8-9)

(vi) The Bible says that God would forgive our iniquity and sin (Psalm 32:5, 6; 51: 1 – 19.)

(vii) For us to receive forgiveness of our sins, we must confess and forsake them. (John 5:14; 8:11)

(viii) We cannot hide our sins – (Proverbs 28:13; 1 John 1:9.)

(ix) The Bible further states, that, it is the Blood of Jesus that cleanses us from all sin (1 John 1:7.) It assures us that God removes our sins from us as far as the East is from the West (Psalm 103:12) and forgets them (Isaiah 43:25 and Jeremiah 31: 34).

4

Deliverance from

Demonic influence

As Christians, we sometimes have things in our lives that keep us in bondage: sins, sickness, "weights" (Hebrews 12:1), etc. Demonic influence sometimes causes these things. However, sometimes they are caused by lack of knowledge, poor eating habits (as in the case of some sicknesses), the refusal to crucify your flesh, etc. It is our desire in this study, to show from the Scriptures, how you can receive your deliverance in the case where demons/unclean Spirit influence your bondage.

"...for of whom a man is overcome, of the same is he brought into bondage."– (2 Peter 2:19)

"Wherefore seeing we also are compassed about with so great a cloud of witnesses, let us lay aside every weight, and the sin which doth so easily beset us, and let us run with patience the race that is set before us." (Hebrews 12:1)

"And, behold, there was a woman who had a spirit of infirmity eighteen years, and was bowed together, and could in no wise lift up herself. And when Jesus saw her,

he called her to him, and said unto her, "Woman, thou art loosed from thine infirmity."

And he laid his hands on her: and immediately she was made straight, and glorified God. And the ruler of the synagogue answered with indignation, because that Jesus had healed on the Sabbath day, and said unto the people, "There are six days in which men ought to work: in them therefore come and be healed, and not on the Sabbath day."

The Lord then answered him, and said, "Thou hypocrite, doth not each one of you on the Sabbath loose his ox or his ass from the stall, and lead him to watering? And ought not this woman, being a daughter of Abraham, whom Satan hath bound, lo, these eighteen years, be loosed from this bond on the Sabbath day?" (Luke 13: 11 – 16)

The Bible refers to the gods of the nations as devils (Deuteronomy 32:15 - 18) and warns us against bringing their images or jewelry into our homes. Instead, we should destroy them (Deuteronomy 7: 25 – 26; 1 Corinthians 10: 20 - 22.)

Demonic Practices Forbidden

God warns about satanic/ demonic practices in Deuteronomy 18: 9 -12. "Let no-one be found among you who sacrifices his son or daughter in the fire, who practices divination or sorcery, interprets omens, engages in witchcraft, or cast spells, or who is a medium or spiritist or who consults the dead" (NIV).

God hates Witchcraft because it ultimately destroys our children and family. "And they abandoned all the commandments of the LORD their God, and made for themselves metal images of two

14

calves, and they made an Asherah and worshiped all the host of heaven and served Baal. And **they burned their sons and their daughters as offerings** and used divination and omens and sold themselves to do evil in the sight of the LORD, provoking him to anger. Therefore, the LORD was very angry with Israel and removed them out of his sight. None was left but the tribe of Judah only". (2Kings 17:16-18)

In some witchcraft practice, the covenant has to make, confirm or ratify on the offering up as a sacrifice the firstborn. "When the king of Moab saw that the battle was going against him, he took with him 700 swordsmen to break through, opposite the king of Edom, but they could not. **Then he took his oldest son who was to reign in his place and offered him for a burnt offering on the wall.** And there came great wrath against Israel. And they withdrew from him and returned to their own land". (2 Kings 3:26, 27)

Paul warns us with a do not, "Take no part in the unfruitful works of darkness, but instead expose them. For it is shameful even to speak of the things that they do in secret". (Ephesian 5:11, 12)

Definition of selected words (Deuteronomy 18: 9 - 14)

• _To pass through the fire:_ – To offer as sacrifice a person to an idol/demon as an act of worship. To perform as a ritualistic act dedicated to an idol/ god or devil.

• _Witchcraft:_ – To control a person against their will through sorcery, spells/and incantations and magic. To play with a person's emotion as a means to control them.

• _Soothsayer:_ - one who tries to tell the future using divination, clairvoyance, dreams, and fortune telling, etc.; a psychic.

• *Omen:* - an event regarded as a prophetic sign from the gods or from someone that is dead, or lucky charms; the reading of stars, crystals, tarot cards and tea leaf, etc. That is seen as good or bad luck. E.g., that which is being used in the lottery gaming /gambling industry in Jamaica, commonly called "rake."

• *Sorcerer* (wizard): - a male witch. In Jamaica, this would be an Obeah-man, Reader-man, Talisman or Balm Yard man, Kuminah and or myal-men Priest. The female equivalent to this which is a Witch, in Jamaica is known as a "Mother" or "Reader woman" and "Healer."

• *To Conjure up spells*: - to attack a person by evil means or using a demon spirit to inflict harm to a person through chants, oils, powder, poison and specially recited words, e.g., voodoo dolls.

• *Necromancer*: someone who calls up the spirit of the dead.

• *Necromancy* - is the act calling up the dead using séances, myal (or myalism) feast or Kuminah/ poco party.

We (the Believers) have been given authority to tread (walk) upon all the power of the enemy, and nothing will hurt us – (Matthew 10:1; Luke 10: 19.)

God has promised to deliver us from our enemies and not our friends; therefore, we must hate all satanic activity – (Luke 1: 71, 74; Proverbs 3: 7.)

God expects us to cast out devils in the name of Jesus verbally – (Matthew 8: 16; Mark 16: 17.)

16

Steps to receiving and keeping your deliverance

(i) Confess any known sin (1 John 1: 9, Proverbs 26: 13).

(ii) To renounce, i.e., to give up by actual, formal declaration, any involvement, believes, practice and or adherence to the teachings of these things that God forbids; give up the things which give Satan access to your life.eg. Guard rings, horoscope, balm-yard/revivalism and gambling, Ouija boards, tarot cards, the use of dream books and the oaths and covenants made to secret societies and lodges– (Acts 8:9-24; 19:13-20)

In Isaiah God said this. "Because you have said, "We have made a covenant with death, and with Sheol (the underworld) we have an agreement, when the overwhelming whip passes through it will not come to us, for we have made lies our refuge, and in falsehood, we have taken shelter."; Therefore thus says the Lord GOD, "Behold, I am the one who has laid as a foundation in Zion, a stone, a tested stone, a precious cornerstone, of a sure foundation: 'Whoever believes will not be in haste.' And I will make justice the line, and righteousness the plumb line; and hail will sweep away the refuge of lies, and waters will overwhelm the shelter." Then your covenant with death will be annulled (canceled), and your agreement with Sheol (the underworld) will not stand; when the overwhelming scourge (another way to say his judgment) passes through, you will be beaten down by it. (Isaiah 28:15-18) ESV.

(iii) Demand your release from demonic influence in Jesus' name (Acts 16: 18, Mark 11: 23, Mark 16: 17).

(iv) You may need someone to pray with you, i.e., take you through a deliverance process/ Session – (James 5:14-16.)

(v) Determine in your heart through faith that you will not go back to the thing God deliver you. Galatians 5:1 says "For freedom

Christ has set us free; stand firm therefore, and do not submit again to a yoke of slavery." ESV.

(vi) Present your body as a living sacrifice, holy and acceptable to the lord. (i.e., as suitable place for God to dwell) (Romans 12:1,2; 1Corintians 6:13,15-20; Galatians 5:1921)

(vii) Fill your life with God's Word (Matthew12: 43 – 45, Psalms 119: 9 - 11)

(viii) Renew your mind (intellect, emotion, and Will) as well as the spirit (attitude) of your mind with the truth of God's word (Romans 12:2; Ephesians 4:17-32 Psalm 119:9)

(ix) Break your love affair/addiction with the world (1 John 2:15-17)

(x) Seek to become Holy Spirit Guided and lead (Romans 8:1,4; Galatians 5:16,25)

5

Empowered by The Holy Spirit

For us to understand and appreciate the work of the Holy Spirit we need to learn more about the Godhead. The Bible teaches that God is triune. Here it shows that the Godhead is made up of three distinct persons who are equal in every way.

Please note I said persons and not *personalities,* as the word personality implies that God has schizophrenia.

We, therefore, believe, as the Bible teaches, that there is one God, yet He reveals Himself as Father, Son, and Holy Spirit. Genesis 1:1- 3, 26, 27; John 1: 1-4, here we see God introduce Himself as *Elohim* which is the plural word for God. The singular word for God is "El."

This would make verses 26 and 27 of Genesis chapter 2 read like this: "Elohim (Father, Son, and Holy Spirit) said, "Let us make mankind in our image ...." "So God (Elohim) created man in His own (singular personal pronoun) image.... He created him male and female created He them". This is further borne out in the Jewish Shema (shaw-mah), Article of faith number one, found in Deuteronomy 6: 4-9. Here we read "Hear O Israel, the Lord our God" or "Jehovah Elohim (e·lo·hei·nu) is one (e·chad.) Lord."

All three revealed persons were involved in creation – (John 1:1-4; Colossians 1:15-18; Genesis1:1-2, 26, and 27.)

All three revealed persons were involved in redemption – (2 Corinthians 5:19 -26; Colossians 1: 19-22)

All three revealed persons are involved in sanctification – (John 17: 17-19; Acts.10:38.)

There is nothing that happens in the earth which is done by God in which all three revealed persons are not involved.

The Father is revealed in the following ways, in the Old Testament: -

- The Father is featured as the initiator of creation "Let us make man" (Genesis 1:26)
- The Father is shown as the One who made himself of one man a nation for Himself. (Genesis 12:2, 35:11)
- The father is established as the lawgiver. (Exodus 34:28; Deuteronomy 4:13)
- The father is typified as the Father who would sacrifice His own son, as is seen in the account of Abraham and Isaac. (Genesis 22:10-14.)
- In the New Testament, the Father is revealed as the Great Judge whose justice must be appeased (Romans 3:6; 11Thomoty 4:1, 8 Hebrews10:30; 12:32; 9: 22.)

The Son/Jesus was revealed in the following ways:

- The Son (Jesus) is featured as the word released in (Genesis chapter 1:3 as "and God said" St John 1:1-4)
- The son was also shown as the Passover lamb in the book of Exodus. (Exodus 12:13, 27; 34:25)
- The son was typified as the blood sacrifices offered on altars built to God – (Hebrews 10: 1-10.)

- The Son took on flesh (Jesus) and appeased the Father's justice by dying on a cross by crucifixion (Mathew 20:28; John 3:14-19; 19: 17 – 42; 1Peter 2: 21, 24.)

The Holy Spirit is revealed in the following ways.

- The Holy Spirit is featured as the one that moved upon the face of the deep (Genesis 1:2)
- The Holy Spirit is typified as the fire that sits on the Prophets, spurring/stirring them to speak as they were carried along under His influence – (2 Peter 1: 20, 21.)
- The Holy Spirit is revealed as the One who leads into all truth; Counselor; Comforter; Baptizer of Fire; Bride Preparer and Down Payment to our total redemption (Mathew 3:11 John.14:16-17; Acts 1:8; 2:1- 4. Ephesians 1:13; 3:5; 4: 30; 1 Thessalonians 4:8)

His purpose for coming

(i) He is a Person, not a thing or an "it." (As in Romans 8:16 and 26 which is poor translation in the King James Version of the Bible from the original text)

(ii) Jesus said of the Holy Spirit John 16:13 "Howbeit when he, the Spirit of truth, is come, he will guide you into all truth: for He shall not speak of himself; but whatsoever He shall hear, that shall he speak: and he will show you things to come." KJV.

(iii) He has emotions (the ability to feel) (Romans 8:26 (NKJV); Ephesians 4:30)

(iv) He has an Intellect (intelligence, ability to reason) (1 Timothy 4:1, Acts 16:7) and

(v) He has a Will (ability to make decisions) (Acts 13:2; 1 Corinthians 12:11.)

21

Examples of His activities in the Scriptures

- His work in creation – (Genesis 1: 2.)
- He was responsible for Joseph's ability to interpret dreams – (Genesis 41: 38.)
- He gave the Judges supernatural abilities – (Judges 6: 34, 11: 29; 14: 5 – 6.)
- He inspired and spoke through the Prophets (Ezekiel 11: 5; Revelation 1: 10.)
- He is the true or actual author of the holy scriptures (2 Timothy 3:16; 2 Peter 1:21)

Some phrases used to describe Him in the Old Testament

Isaiah 11: 2

- The Spirit of the Lord
- The Spirit of Wisdom
- The Spirit of Understanding
- The Spirit of Counsel
- The Spirit of Might
- The Spirit of Knowledge
- The Spirit of the Fear of the Lord

Zechariah 12:10

- The Spirit of Grace

His work in the Believer's life

- He is responsible for the new birth and confirmation of our relationship with God – (John 3: 5 – 6; Romans 8: 15 – 16; Galatians 4: 6.)

- He teaches us, leads us into all truths and shows us things to come – (John 14: 26, 16: 13.)
- He empowers us for service – (Micah 3:8; Acts 1: 8; John 14: 12.)
- We also read in John "And I will ask the Father, and He will give you another Comforter *(Counselor, Helper, Intercessor, Advocate, Strengthener, and Standby)* that He may remain with you forever." (John 14: 16) (Amp.)

The Baptism of the Holy Spirit

- God, the Father has promised to give to us the Holy Spirit who, when He comes, will give us power (Greek – dunamis: dynamite, dynamic, dynamo, etc.) (Acts 1: 4 – 8.)
- We would be clothed with power from on high – (Luke 24: 49.)
- The promise of the Holy Spirit is to all God's children – (Luke 11:13; Acts 2: 38 – 39.)
- The Scriptures are quite clear that a man can be saved and experience the baptism in the Holy Spirit – (Acts 8: 12 – 17; Acts 19: 1 – 6.)
- The Holy Spirit is received by faith – (Galatians 3: 2 – 5.)
- The Bible encourages us that when we pray we should believe that we receive (or that our request is granted to us) and we would have it – (Mark 11: 24.)
- The Bible promises that if we ask we will receive – (Luke 11: 9 – 10.)

In every recorded incident of people experiencing the Baptism in the Holy Spirit two distinct things occur:
- They drink and flow (John 7: 37 – 38.)
- They were filled and spoke (Acts 2: 4.)

- The Holy Spirit falling on the Believers and they spoke out in tongues. (Acts 10: 44 – 46)
- The Holy Spirit came on them, and they spoke. (Acts 19: 6)

From the Scriptures mentioned above, it is clear that the initial evidence of the baptism in the Holy Spirit is the ability to speak in other tongues. Critics of the baptism of the Holy Spirit say the Bible teaches that tongues and prophecies will cease therefore these gifts are passed with the Apostles – (1 Corinthians 13:8.)

They, however, fail to see that it also said "knowledge will pass away," and despite that, we still have 'knowledge' and are still speaking. They will also tell you that we are living in the last days, but they ignore Joel's prophecy which says that it is in the last days that God said He, "I will pour out my Spirit" (Joel 2: 28, 29.) We are still in the last days.

There is no danger whatsoever of a Believer receiving a demon spirit or false tongues – (Luke 11: 11 – 13.)

The Holy Spirit's effect on our lives (The Gifts and Fruit)

Contained in the book First Corinthians a list of the "gifts" of the Holy Spirit is given. (1 Corinthians 12: 8 – 10.) The following listed below are examples from other Scriptures of them in operation: -

(i) Tongues (Acts 2: 4 - 11.)
(ii) Interpretation (Daniel 5: 25 – 28.)
(iii) Prophecy (2 Kings 22: 15 – 20.)
(iv) Working of miracles (2 Kings 6: 1 – 7; John 2: 1 – 9.)
(v) Faith (Mark 11: 12 – 14, Mark 5: 25 – 34.)
(vi) Healing (Matthew 8: 14 – 17.)
(vii) Word of wisdom (Genesis 41: 33 – 36.)
(viii) Word of knowledge (2 Kings 6: 8 – 12.)

(ix) Discerning of spirits (2 Kings 6: 17, Acts 16: 16 – 18.)

The "gifts" are available to each Believer who is baptized in the Holy Spirit (1Corinthians 12:7, 11; John 14:12), and we allow them to manifest through us by faith (Galatians 3: 5; Romans 12:6).

The gifts are supposed to follow us, not the other way around. – (Mark 16: 17.)

There is a more excellent way to minister the "gifts" of the Holy Spirit. It is called the way of love. – (1 Corinthians 12:31. Galatians 5: 22 – 23) "But the fruit of the Spirit is love, joy, peace, longsuffering, gentleness, goodness, faith, meekness, temperance: against such, there is no law."

(Luke 6:44) - "For every tree is known by his own fruit..."

The Gifts of the Holy Spirit are supposed to be influenced by love and compassion. – (Matthew 14: 14; 1 Corinthians 13: 1-2; Galatians 5: 6.)

We, therefore, believe that the Baptism of the Holy Spirit is the Blood- purchased right of every true born-again Believer. (Acts 2:39) We believe that in this experience lies the necessary empowerment one needs for the effective evangelizing of the nations in the preaching of the Gospel with signs and wonders and miracles following. (Acts1:8; 2:1- 47; 10 38; 2 Corinthians 3:5; 4:7.)

6

Growing in Our Relationship with God

Prayer is literally mean talking to God and listening to Him speaks to us by His Word and the witness of the Holy Spirit.

The phrase, "when ye pray" implies that Jesus expects us to pray – (Matthew 6: 5-9.)

The Lord expects us to "pray without ceasing" (Luke 18: 1; Ephesians 6: 18) and we should always approach each prayer session with a heart of praise and thanksgiving – (Matthew 6: 9; 1 Corinthians 1: 4, Philippians 4: 6.)

God's Attitude towards a Christian's Prayer

- "…but the prayer of the upright is His delight." (Proverb 15: 8b)
- "…He hears the prayer of the righteous." (Proverb 15: 29b)
- "… and you go and pray unto me, and I will hear you. (Jeremiah 29:12, 13)
- "For the eyes of the Lord are over the righteous, and His ears are open unto their prayers…" (1 Peter 3: 12)
- If we have no respect for God's Word our prayers will not be acceptable before God – (Proverb 28: 9.)
- Broken relationships and a heart that will not forgive others can hinder our prayers (1 Peter 3:7); and we are instructed to mend

them before we come to God in prayer. (Matthew 5: 23-24, Mark 11: 25-26).

Listed below are some conditions for answered prayers:

(i)   Humility – (2 Chronicles 7:14.)
(ii) Contrition (Psalm 34:18; 51:17; Isaiah 57:15; 66:2)
(iii) Wholeheartedness – (Jeremiah 29:12-14a.)
(iv) Faith – (Mark 11:24; James 1:6.)
(v)   Obedience – (1 John 3:22.)
(vi) Importunity – (Luke 18:1 – 7; Matthew 11:12.)

The Bible clearly teaches that we are to pray to the Father in the name of Jesus (Matthew 6:6, John 16: 23) and as we pray in accordance with His will we are guaranteed that He will hear our petitions (1John 5: 14 – 15).

The precepts/law of the Lord is good, and it is God's will on any matter it addresses – (Psalm 119: 128.)

Growing through studying the Word

It is essential for us to know that the Bible is not like other books nor should it be referred to as just a good book. The Bible teaches and we believe that it is the inspired word of God. By inspired we mean that God's Breath, or the Holy Spirit as the author, working through holy men in their languages, culture, and personalities, gave man the very word of God without omission or error. We can verify the credibility of the Old Testament (Genesis to Malachi) just from the fact that Jesus quoted it, taught it, endorsed it, and lived it, calling it Scripture. (Luke 4:16-21; Hebrews 10:7.)

The New Testament has its validity by the fact that those who wrote it were eyewitnesses who experienced the ministry of Jesus and or His Apostles. Jesus himself said, "A new covenant/testament I give unto you." (Matthew 26:28; Mark 14:24; Luke 22:20; 1John 1:1 -7; 2 Thessalonians 3:16, 17.)

The Bible has a 100% success rate on the fulfillment of all prophecies made in it for which the time has already come for them to be fulfilled.

In Acts 20: 32, we read "And now, brethren, I commend you to God, and to *the Word of His Grace, which is able to build you up*, and to give you an inheritance among all them which are sanctified."

Also, in 2 Timothy 3: 16 – 17 we read "**All scripture is given by inspiration of God**, and is profitable for doctrine, for reproof, for correction, for instruction in righteousness: that the man of God *may be perfect, thoroughly furnished unto all good works."*

These are supported by 1Peter 2: 2 which reads "As newborn babes, desire the sincere milk of the Word that ye may grow thereby."

For us to grow as Christians, we need to feed regularly on God's Word.

In fact, we are reminded that "man does not live by bread alone, but by every word that proceeds from the mouth of God" (Deuteronomy 8:3; Luke 4:4). We are encouraged to study and apply (obey) the Word of God – (2 Timothy 2: 15; James 1: 22.)

The benefits of studying and applying/living the scriptures

- Healing – (Proverb 4: 20 -22.)
- Deliverance – (Psalm 107: 20; John 8: 31-32.)
- Success in all that you put your hand to – (Deuteronomy 28:8; Psalm 1: 1-3; Joshua 1: 8.)

- Renewing of your mind/restoration of your soul (intellect, emotions, and will) – (Psalm 19:7; 1 Peter 1:22.)
- Wisdom and understanding – (Psalm 119: 98 – 100, 105.)
- Sanctification or keeping us clean before God – (Psalm 119: 9 – 11; John 17:17.)
- Faith strengthened – (Romans 10: 17.)
- Fellowship with God strengthened – (John 14: 21, 23.)
- Guarantee of answered prayers – (John 15:1; John 3: 22.)
- Spiritual growth – (Acts 20:32; 1Peter 2:2.)

How to have an effective personal Bible study

(i) Procure a good Bible for yourself - King James and New King James versions, Revised Standard Version, New International Version, etc.

(ii) Set aside a time and place to spend in the Scriptures (although reading the Bible while on the bus etc. would be good). (2 Timothy 2:15)

(iii) Pray for God's guidance as you read – (James 1: 5.)

(iv) Start small and increase over time – (Isaiah 28: 10.)

(v) A good place to start is in the New Testament, and after you have gone through it a few times then the whole Bible.

(vi) Use a notebook and jot down any relevant thoughts you may have while reading the Scriptures.

(vii) Underline or highlight passages that "come alive" while you are reading.

(viii) Use Bible studies aids, concordances etc.

(ix) Share what you learn with others.

There are three basic ways most people study the Bible: -

   a) Book by book, e.g., Genesis, Exodus, etc.

b) Character study e.g... David, Joseph, etc. and

c) A topic by topic study, e.g., prayer, the Second coming of Christ, etc.

How to make The Bible come alive

The job of interpreting the Bible has been a source of frustration for a lot of Christians, and therefore some persons don't bother to read the Bible as they say they "can't understand it."

The Basic Rules That Govern The Interpretation Of The Bible

Before giving the rules, let me make a few things clear. There are certain rules or laws that govern the extraction / unfolding (interpretation) of information from the Bible, and these must be observed. One cannot say, "Well, the Holy Spirit tell me an' a so it go"! (Jamaican vernacular) There must be a clear Biblical or Bible-based evidence that the conclusions arrived at are consistent with the overall teaching/truth taught in the scriptures.

One must also remember that interpretation comes before application; therefore, our interpretation will shape the accuracy with which we live our lives. This then is the principle, *"interpretation affects understanding, understanding affects application, application affects results/success and success affects our love walk with the Lord"* (Wayne Palmer)

Rule No. 1: When you go to the Bible to study and hear from God, don't go with your mind fixed with the answer already, but go open and teachable so that God may fill you with His truth and knowledge.

Rule No. 2: Do not yield to the temptation of twisting the Scripture to match your wrongdoing or sin. e.g., drinking strong drinks then saying, "The Bible says I must drink wine for the stomach's sake." (1 Timothy 5:23); or a person who is in an intimate relationship with two or three females, along with the person God gave them in engagement or marriage, saying, "Solomon had more than one wife."

Rule No. 3: Do not add or take away from the Bible; that is, do not put meaning to the Bible that is not there, nor is implied there; neither you make light, down-play (water down) the interpretation - (Revelation 22:18, 19).

Rule No. 4: Let the Bible speak (interpret) for itself; i.e., use the Bible to explain the Bible. Remember, the Old Testament is the New Testament concealed or hidden, and the New Testament is the Old Testament revealed or made plain. In other words, from what we see happening or acted out in the New Testament, we can go back to the Old Testament and find the reasons and principles why the thing happened the way it did or why the act was done in the way it was.

Rule No. 5: When interpreting a passage, first look at the verse or passage in its context. The context here means, how does this verse fit in with what was said in the verses before and the verses that come after the verse in focus; if it is still not clear, look at how that verse fits in the whole chapter, and in the book (the overall message).

Rule No. 6: When seeking to find the meaning of a word in a passage, first look at what was said before and after the word. If you are still not clear, then consider it in light of what was said a few verses before and after.

If you are still not clear, you may need to do what is called, an "etymology" or word study. This means in studying a word you will need to go back to that word first usage, origin or roots to find its meaning. E.g., the word "conversation" in 1Timothy 4:12 which has the word, "word" coming before it. This means that "conversation" could not mean, "To converse" or "dialogue." A word study would reveal that it means, "Behavior /lifestyle" or "one's way of life."

Rule No. 7: Whenever one word appears twice in a passage, it does not always carry or have the same meaning. This is so because some words are masculine or feminine etc.; also, the parts of speech may be different from our regular parts of speech. This should be made clear by your word study.

A word study is done by using well research Bible dictionary that specializes in how words are used in an accent text and context. (e.g., Strong's Exhaustive Concordance) Instead of an ordinary English dictionary, as most dictionaries look at words as a current word with current meaning and in their present usage. Bible dictionaries not only look at the meanings of a word but its root, gender, part of speech, etc. as it comes across languages it uses then and possible use now. A Bible dictionary may be bought at a Christian bookstore also you may be able to do this word study online. (May I recommend www.BibleHub.com)

Rule No. 8: There are some fundamental questions to be asked when approaching/ interpreting a passage.

Who? - Who is doing the speaking and who did He say the things to? Who was He writing to, (what people)? (e.g., the message to the seven churches in Revelation chapters 2 and 3) Was it to them only, or does apply to me also?

What? - What was God or the author saying in this passage back then? What is God saying to me now? What was the historical and cultural background to this text? For this, you may need an excellent Bible Commentary

Why? - Why did God or the author say it this way? Why did He not say something else? Why must a thing be done in that way?

When? - When was it said/spoken? When is it going to happen? This is especially true as it relates to prophecies. E.g. Joel 2:28

How? - How did God say it must be done? (e.g. 2Chronicle 7:14) How did it affect the then hearers and how will it affect me now reading it?

Where? - Where was it done? (e.g. Jesus' arrest or the place of an event) Where did it take place? Where must I do it?

These questions help you to find background information and the answers you need to know in understanding the text.

Rule No. 9: Begin Bible study by choosing a topic for the week or month. Keep a notepad along with a pencil or pen to make notes as you read. Do not be afraid to mark in your Bible. It is not a sin.

Rule No. 10: Pay attention to sermons, especially sermons with systematic teaching, and note the different explanations to the passages used by the Speakers. Ask the Holy Spirit to guide you, for He is the Teacher and Revealer of the secret things of God.

7

Growing through Thanksgiving, Praise, and Worship

Thanksgiving – *is an expression of gratitude or appreciation.* Thanksgiving begins with giving thanks for the small things such as His (God's) goodness and His mercies (2 Samuel 22:50; 1Chronicles 16:34; Psalm 18:49; 105:1.) The Bible lists this as a necessary preparation for entering even the church gates and grounds (courts) (Psalm 100:4.)

Praise – is *to express warm approval or admiration, and (b) to glorify God in words.* We are encouraged to offer praise and thanksgiving to God (Psalm 22:23, Psalm105:1, Ps 106:1.) We should remember that praise focuses on the hands of God in three dimensions, that is, *on what He has done, what He is now doing* and *what He is going to do* - (past, present, and future).

How we should praise and thank the Lord

- By speaking – (Luke 19:37; Psalm 51:15.)
- By shouting – (Ezra 3:11; Psalm 100:1; Psalm 132:16)
- By singing – (Psalm 100:2; Psalm 69:30.)
- With instruments – (Psalm 33:2; Psalm 150:3 – 5.)
- With the lifting up of our hands – (Psalm 134:2; Psalm 63:4.)
- With dancing – (Psalm 150:4; Psalm 149: 3.)
- With the clapping of our hands – (Psalm 47:1)

- We should offer praise at all times   - (Psalm 34:1) and
- In all circumstances – (1 Thessalonians 5: 18.)
- In fact, praise is a command, not a suggestion. (Psalm 150:6)

The ascending levels of Praise

As we look at what is commonly called the seven (7) levels of praise, I hope that it will propel you and reveal Christ high and lifted up. The kind of revelation that will not only change you but everyone that is associated with you.

1) Todah (תּוֹדָה) to-daw'

This occurrence: 32 times in the KLV as Thanksgiving, 17; praise, 5; thank, 3

- Todah: - The sacrifice of Praise or thank giving

Todah is the first level the priest had to learn in the Old Testament economy. It was not only needed then but is more so needed now as the hustle and bustle of our world today sometimes leaves us not being ready worshipers.

Todah means "The sacrifice of praise." It is thanksgiving for what God is going to do. This speaks of a deliberate act of the will (a decision) on the part of the worshiper. Psalm56:12b says, "I will render praises unto thee" (emphasis added).

David said as a part of paying his vows he would render (I will pay or re-pay) his praise. Psalm 50:23 said, "Whoso offereth praise glorifieth me: and to him that ordereth his conversation aright will I show the salvation of God." KJV

The hint in this passage is that this kind of praise rearranges our priorities. That is: we should not be in a pasture of worship, and our mind is somewhere else, our spirit struggling to give a worthy praise

35

and our bodies tired. We should command our souls to Todah the Lord. On some of the times that this method of praise is used in the book of Psalms you would see the phrase "I will." Imagine David saying "I will bless the Lord at all times..." Someone may say it is not possible to praise the Lord in every situation, but with this approach of praise, we can. Will you?

Other passages to look at are (Psalm 69:30; 68:4, 75:9, Jeremiah 17:26.)

This is the kind of praise we bring to the house of the Lord.

2) Yadah (ידה) Ya-daw'

This Occurrence: 114 times in the KJV as praise, 52; thanks, 32; confess, 11; thank, 4; confessed, 3

Yadah: - The sacrifice of Praise or thank giving with a quick voluntary throw of your hands upward in the air.

Yadah is the second level of praise that was taught and is one of the most common words used in the scripture to mean Praise. It is also the root word from which other words of praise get their origin. Yadah, like Todah, means a sacrifice of thanksgiving, with an emphasis on the throwing out of the hands in the air in public or private worship.

- In Psalm 118:21 David said: "I will praise (Yadah) thee because you have heard my cry..." (Todah is implied) "...and have become my salvation." Let's paraphrase this passage by using the meaning we already know. I will throw (Yadah) my hands in the air as a sacrifice of thanksgiving at the time of public worship because while I was praising (Todah), you responded to me with your deliverance. Wow!

36

Yadah also means axle, an axle is that on which a wheel is turned. This means that when we praise, things get turned around in our lives.

- Yadah also has its meaning, authority. Our praise releases the authority/power in and from God over the world, the flesh, and the devil, rendering them powerless. There are over 20 times that this praise is used to imply confession to God about our own sins. (Leviticus 5:5; 16:21; Numbers 5: 7; Ezekiel 10:1; Proverbs 28:13.)

Here are some of the other places where this word was used - meditate on them:

- Out of a love-less marriage Le'ah cried at the birth of her fourth son, "Now I will praise the Lord" (Genesis 29:35.)
- "I will yet praise him who is the health of my countenance and my God." (Psalm 43:5.)
- "I will praise the Lord with my whole heart, in the assembly of the upright, and in the congregation." (Psalm 111: 1.)
- "I will freely praise you" (Psalm 54:6.)
- "I will greatly praise the Lord" (Psalm 109:30.)

The throwing out of the hands is always a sign of surrender. When done towards God, we are saying "the battle is yours oh Lord, not mine," and "Yes Lord, not my will but yours be done."

3) Halal (הלל) Haw-lal'

This occurrence: 166 times in the KJV as praise, 92 .It is the root from which the word Halleluiah comes.

This is a demonstration of praise that I would love to see become more common in the church and in particular among the leaders in the churches. Why you may ask?   The reason is that many have forgotten the freshness of the fire of their coming to the Lord and have become so 'pious' and sometimes callous in their posture of praise to God.

Halal means "to boast, to shine, celebrate to be clear, to be clamorously foolish." In the words of the late Dr. Myles Munroe "To stop being cute and be righteous."

Halal also means "to be insane" - 1 Samuel 21:13 "fools" or "foolish"; (Job 12:17; Psalm73:3.)

The suggestions from these meanings are as follows:

- God is looking for certain abandonment from His worshipers, but sometimes we are too sophisticated, too dignified, and too inflexible. Psalm 107:32 says, "Praise Him in the assembly of the elders." Elders were the leaders of the home, community and later on in the New Testament leaders in the church. God is saying that people in leadership should be clamorously foolish before Him among the congregation. Why is this so important? I believe it's because it strips us of pride and makes us no longer self-conscious, and man-conscious, but God-conscious.

Here are some other references to where this kind of praise has been done openly publicly.
- Psalm 35:18 "I will praise Him among the people."
- Psalm 109:30b "I will praise you among the multitude."
- Psalm 115:17 "…the dead do not praise the Lord."
- David said seven times a day do I praise you. (Psalm 119:164.)
- It ought to be done with joyful lips (Psalm 63:5.) "I will praise God by praising His word," (Psalm 56:4, 10.)

- Jesus said, "I will declare thy name unto my brethren; in the midst of the congregation will I praise thee." (Psalm 22:22; Hebrews 2:12.)

Halal, having been used no less than 166 times in the Bible, as well as been the root from which the word Halleluiah is derive, I can safely say;

I believe God is trying to get our attention, don't you?

4) Zamar (זמר)Zaw-mar'
   This occurrence: 42 in the KJV as; sing, 36; praise, 4

Zamar

This is the fourth demonstration of praise that was known to the worshipers of that day. Zamar means to touch the strings of a musical instrument and is usually accompanied by the vocalists.

This level also connotes an instrumental praise (Psalm 150) and dance (Psalm149:3). This shows to us that God expects us to understand that we can climb into three dimensions of praise without a single note being played on an instrument. That's when a so-called "worshiper" emerges from a service in which the musicians did not remember to attend and says "that church was boring." It is not the musicians who are at fault; it is purely the failure of the worshiper's heart that is responsible. You see, when a person is truly passionate towards God he or she doesn't need music to get him or her to praise Him. Music, then, is as an extension to his/her praise, an accompaniment. A means by which one extends the excitement that he or she already has towards God.

Look at David's heart in Psalm 108:1-2. He said "My heart is steadfast" (or "fixed"). You may ask "Fixed on what?"

1) *Fixed* on his love walk with the Lord
2) *Fixed* on giving the Lord thanks for what he has done
3) *Fixed* on His commitment to seeking the Lord early in the morning
4) *Fixed* on getting so close to God he could hear Him speak

Notice it was his heart in worship, and not his skill to play, although he was a very skilled musician. When his heart was engaged in worship, he then awakens his instruments to join him in praise to God. They, in turn, help to awaken the morning to join him in praise to God. David did not wait for the music to awaken him in the morning so that they could praise God.

Psalm 150: 6 said, "Let everything that hath breath praise the Lord." David said even in the face of blatant idolatry "I will still praise (Zamar) you and worship toward your Holy temple" Psalm 138:1-2. This is because his heart was fixed (Psalm 57: 7-8.) Finally, David said 'we will sing and praise thy power" (Psalm 21: 13.)

5) Shabach (שבח) shaw-bakh'
   This occurrence: 11 times in the KLV as praise, 4; commended, 1; triumph, 1

Shabach

This is the fifth dimension of praise so let me warn you that if you belong to the church of the chosen frozen, this kind of praise is guaranteed to shake up things in you. A key thing to remember is that praise is always expressive and cannot be done silently. Let me explain if you were to think highly of someone and never let the person know, what good would that do to the person? Have you ever imagined what it would have been like if the woman who washed

Jesus' feet with her hair and anointed them with that precious perfume, had just burst the door open and then stood there staring at him?

Shabach means, "To command, triumph, to address with or in a loud tone, to glory or glorify." In what is referred to in scripture as the 'triumphal entry of Jesus' found in Luke 19: 37-38. It showed that the people praised God in a loud voice in acknowledgment of Jesus. That crowd must have been charged with an attitude of gratitude so that not even the Pharisees could stop them. Jesus' response to the Pharisees' request was, "if these people hold their peace then the rocks and stones shall cry out."

We address the Lord in a loud tone not because He is deaf but because we love Him, we love his victory over our enemy, and he said we address him that way. A church member would go to football /soccer match, cheer like they are crazy because their team scored a goal but would sit in a church like wooden statues and turn up their noses at someone giving a triumphal praise to the Lord.

When we are giving our testimony, i.e., testifying (praising) God's work to others (another generation), Shabach (to speak aloud) is how it should be done – (Psalm145:4.) Why should we Shabach? We should do so because of His loving-kindness which is better than life - Psalm 63:3. We should Shabach him because He is God, also because He is our strength, our grace and He blesses our children. (Psalm147:12-14)

The early church made Shabach a regular part of their fellowship. (Acts 2:46-47; 3:8.) Shabach is the kind of praise that is featured around the throne. (Rev. 5:12; 6:10; 7:10.)

May God loose you from people's approval to God's approval in your giving of praise unto Him.

6) Barak (בָּרַךְ) baw-rak'

This occurrence: 324 in the KJV as blessed, 176; bless, 116; praise

Barak – (Judges 5:2-3)

This is the sixth dimension of praise exposed in the scripture as a way that we should minister to the Lord. Barak means "to kneel, to bless, to praise" and implies to prostrate oneself. To wait in quietness and expectancy after all the other levels that went up to Him. We now get to the place where things are about to change suddenly as God begins His introduction to us of the act of worship. We need Barak to hear God. We can't be doing all the talking in this relationship; He wants to speak in prophecy, word of wisdom and word of knowledge.

There is a place to be quiet, Barak. When a woman is pregnant, we say that she is expecting. Barak means, to be expectant in a spiritual sense, it is to be pregnant with faith and hope. We do not hope for what we already have. To be expectant in a praise sense is to believe that through the act of our praise we would get God's full attention and results beyond our wildest imagination. (Ephesians 3:20)

Barak also means "to bless." How can we bless the Lord in a time of silence before Him? We do so by not forgetting His benefits. The old Saints used to say: "He satisfies." There is a way of blessing that is released to us in this act of praising God so we, in turn, can bless our fellow man. (Genesis 9:26; Deuteronomy 1:10.)

God himself indicates the kind of blessing (Barak) He gives to His people in Genesis 1:22. He blesses with fruitfulness and multiplication, (Genesis. 9:1.) God blesses (Barak) us with the things we eat, with joy, by providing for you and your family,

(Deuteronomy 12:7.) He makes you fairer than the sons of men and pours grace on your lips, (Psalm 45: 2.)

The priest of God would speak this blessing (Barak) over the people of God, saying: "God will bless (Barak) your bread and your water, take away sickness from you, and see to it that you do not suffer miscarriages, nor will you or your children be barren. His fear would go before you and drive out your enemy"- (Exodus 23:25-27.)

Let us Barak the Lord and silence our enemies.

7) Tehillah (הלהת) teh-hil-law'

This occurrence: 57 in the KJV as, Praise, 52; praises, 5;

Tehillah

There is so much to say about this level of praise. This is the seventh dimension, and it is the most underutilized among the Jamaican church. It is the praise that has been squeezed out of the Church by tightly inflexibly planned programs, by the traditions of men, by uninformed pastors and church leaders, and by our unwillingness to please God rather than man.

Tehillah is used about 57 times in the Bible. It means a new song. In Psalm 40:3, David said: "He put a new song in my mouth Tehillah praise) unto our God, many shall see and fear and put their trust in the Lord." Note the "b" section Tehillah is defined as a song that can be seen. The song that evangelizes by revealing Christ as highly exalted, this song (praise) is the lost evangelism tool of the church. "Many shall see and fear /revere and put their trust in the Lord."

Tehillah is the only praise of the seven which the Bible tells us God inhabits or lives in or is enthroned upon. (Psalm 22:3.)

In the New Testament Tehillah is called an 'ode of the Spirit.' (Ephesians 5:19-20,1Corinthians 14:15.) It is something that the early church was known to have practiced even while they were being burnt at the stake, or thrown to lions.

Tehillah is also the end of our faith praise, as God has responded by His presence literally dwelling in and on our praise and invites, draws or releases us into worshiping Him. This praise should be demonstrated, (Psalm 9:14.) This praise should continually be in our mouth (Psalm 34:1; 71:8.) This is the praise that gives us access to the courts of our God (Psalm 100:4.) This praise is described as comely (beautiful). Jehoshaphat used it as a part of his battle plans to defeat his enemy. (2 Chronicles 22:22.) The Bible indicates that God will not share His Tehillah (praise) with another (idols). (Isaiah 42:8, Jeremiah 48:2.)

In the first song attributed to Moses in the scripture, (Exodus 15:11,) the word Tehillah was used to mean "glory" or "glorious." Think about that glory or glorious; this is usually used to describe the dwelling place of God or to describe God Himself. The implication then is that Tehillah is the climate control of our church, in that it creates the atmosphere in which God lives and operates in our midst. This means we get to tell God if He is invited or wanted, and to what extent.

Let us show God that He is welcome, wanted, loved, respected, preferred and absolutely adored. Let's Tehillah the Lord.

Why do we Praise and Thank the Lord

- God said Judah, or "Praise" should go up first. (Judges 1:1, 2)

- Praise unlocks the power of God and releases our promised blessings (Judges 1:1-4; 2 Chronicles 20:21-25)
- It is a powerful weapon of spiritual warfare (Psalm 149:5-9; 2Chronicles 13:9-13)
- It is a major tool for evangelism. (Psalm 40:3)
- Because we are commanded to do so – (Psalm 135:1.)
- Because He is good, merciful and faithful – (Psalm 100:5.)
- Because God is glorified – (Psalm 50:23.)
- Because it releases God's power – (Psalm 67:5-7.)
- It is the way to approach and enter God's Presence, gates and courts (Psalm 100:2, 4; Psalm 95:2)
- It binds the enemy (makes them ineffective) – (Psalm 149:6-9.)

Examples of Praise and Thanksgiving and the results

(i) God's Presence manifested in the temple – (2 Chronicles 5:12-15.)
(ii) Jehoshaphat and Judah being delivered from their enemies– (2 Chronicles 20:20 – 22.)
(iii) Paul and Silas in a Philippian jail – (Acts 16:25-26.)

Worship (חהᴑש) shaw-khaw –

Shachah (Heb.):- To bow down, to prostrate, to fall on knees with forehead touching the ground, to reverence. (Proskuneo Gk):- To kiss towards; to kiss

Worship focuses on the heart of God or on his character. In other words, the Bible's revelation of the things that makes Him distinctly different from all other gods. (Psalm 29:2; 96:9; Revelation 4:10; 5:8, 14.)

Other Definitions: - homage or reverence paid to a deity, adore as divine, idolize or to regard with adoration.

Positions or Postures in Worship

- Kneeling – (Psalm 95:6)
- Bowing – (Psalm 95:6)
- Prostrate on our faces – (Revelation 11:16)
- Humbling ourselves (this should be our attitude)- (Psalm 99:5)
- Holiness or unity - (Psalm 96:9)

Results of spending time waiting on or worshiping God

- We bring him pleasure, as we were created for His pleasure – (Revelation 4:11.)
- It was God's original intent that we should fellowship with Him – (Genesis 3:11)
- We are changed to look like Him who we worship – (Psalm 115:8-11.)
- Our strength is renewed – (Isaiah 40:31.)
- We are transformed into God's image – (2 Corinthians 3:17-18.)
- We receive clear directions from God – (2 Kings 3:15 - 19.)
- Deliverance from demonic spirits – (1 Samuel 16:23; Mark 5:1-13)
- It releases the material, physical and tangible blessings of the Lord- (Luke 4:6,7)

It should be noted that the way God reveals his nature is in his name and the way God unveiled his name is thought the experience we have with him in our day to encounters with challenges, crises, and situation that required his intervention/deliverance. Therefore, these compound names below came out of someone's experience with God, and you will not fully appreciate them until you have walked through something that makes that name impact your life.

Relationship Names of God (Hebrew Names)

Name	*Meaning*	*Scripture Support*
Elohim	Creator God – appears 6823 times in Scriptures	Genesis 1:1; Genesis 6:4
Jehovah (YHVH)	Covenant-making, covenant-keeping God	Exodus 15:26; Exodus 6:3; Psalm 83:18
Jehovah Rapha	The Lord That heals or the lord my physician	Exodus 15:26; Isaiah 53:5
Jehovah Nissi	The Lord my Banner	Exodus 71:8-16
Jehovah Shalom	The Lord is Peace	Judges 6:24
Jehovah Roha or Rohi	The Lord, my Shepherd	Jeremiah 20:6; Psalm 23:1; Psalm 63:11; Isaiah 40:11; John 10:14
Jehovah (tseh –dek) Tsid-ken-u	The Lord our Righteousness	Jeremiah 23:6; 33:16
Jehovah Jireh	The Lord my Provider or the Lord who provides before there is a need	Genesis 22:8, 13
Jehovah Shamma (Sh-awm or Shammah)	The Lord is There	1 Samuel 1:3; Ezek. 48:35
Jehovah Tsebaah (tseb-aw) or Jehovah Sabaoth	The Lord of hosts or The lord of Armies	1Samuel 1:3,11; 2 Samuel 5:10;6:2,18; Psalm 24:10;46:7,11 (Revelation 19:11); Romans 9:29
Jehovah Elyon	The Lord Most High	Psalm 7:17 Psalm 83:18; Psalm 92:8
Jehovah Qadesh (Kadesh)	The Lord who Sanctifies	Leviticus 20:8; Psalm 31:5

Name	Meaning	Scripture Support
Jehovah Elemeth	The Lord of Truth	Numbers 23:19; Titus 1:2; Hebrew 6:18
El Gibor	The Mighty God	Isaiah 9:6
El Shaddai	The Many-Breasted One or God the All-Sufficient One	Genesis 17:1; Isaiah 9:6; Deuteronomy 7:9; Revelation 4:8
El Emunah	The Faithful God	Deuteronomy 32:15; Isaiah 49:7; 1Corinthians 1:9
El Kana	The Jealous God	Deuteronomy 4:24

8

The Burden of Stewardship

Have you ever heard someone say "I will not take my money and give it to a Church or Pastor?" Have you noticed that their life and living conditions get worse and worse and in some cases, for them to survive, have enough, or even look prosperous they have to get involved in shady and/or questionable practices?

God's plan for your success in every area is seen in the principles of giving and receiving, or seed time and harvest time. The truth is God has made you steward over everything He brings into your life whether spiritual or physical, tangible or intangible and economical (meaning enterprise, gifting).

The word "steward" (oikonomas, Gk.) means, a manager or house distributor, an overseer, i.e., an employee in the capacity as fiscal agent (treasurer). Stewardship (oikonomia, Gk.) means, the administration of a household or estate, economy or dispensation.

Stewardship over spiritual things

a) We are made stewards over the mysteries of God (1 Corinthians 4:1)
b) We are made stewards over the manifold grace of God (1 Peter 4:10)
c) We are made stewards over time (Galatians 4:2)
d) We should be wise and faithful stewards (Luke 12:35-48)

e) We have been made stewards of what is not ours; failure to be faithful may stop our success. (Luke 16:1-13)

f) It is a requirement in stewards that they be faithful (1 Corinthians 4:2)

Stewardship over material things

a) God gave the power (anointing, ability, intelligence, and source) to get wealth to establish His Covenant. (Deuteronomy 8:18)

b) Bring all the tithes into the storehouse and prove me (Malachi 3:10)

c) Abram gave a tithe of all to Melchizedek (Genesis. 14:20)

d) Jacob committed himself to the giving of tithes upon his return from Ur of the Chaldeans. (Genesis 28:20)

e) We should take the tithes to the place of worship/storehouse (Numbers 18:26; Malachi 3:10; Nehemiah 10:38; 13:12)

f) The tithes belong to God and if any part is used a fifth part should be added. (Leviticus 27:30-35)

g) Jesus said we should tithe. (Luke 11:42)

Stewardship over first fruits and offerings

a) Honor the Lord with your substance and first fruits (Proverbs 3:9)

b) The first fruit is holy and makes the remainder holy (Romans11:16)

c) The first fruits of a man, animal or harvest belongs to God (Exodus 13:1-2, 12& 13)

d) We should not delay in bringing in the first fruit. (Exodus 22:29; 2 Chronicles 31:5-6)

e) The first fruit is a form of ordinance (Nehemiah 10:35 – 37)

f) Like the tithes, the first fruit should be brought in. (2 Chronicles 31:5-6, 12; Nehemiah. 12:44; 13:5)

g) Our giving unlocks abundance into our lives. (Luke 6:38)

h) We should not rob God's offering. (Malachi 3:8)

What is the first fruit?

There are over fifty (50) passages throughout the Bible that speak of the offering called first fruit. However, there is still some ignorance as to what exactly it is. The best way to understand the first fruit is to remember that the first fruit is always a stated portion /amount in the same way the tithes is a stated portion /amount. In fact, the first fruit is the same amount/percentage as a tithe.

To illustrate this, get ten coins and lay them out in a row to represent the sum total of your first fruit or increase, and then count them from left to right. The first one is the first fruit. To say it another way, if you have a banana field with ten banana trees and one bunch or one tree shows sign of ripening, then that is your entire first fruit of your harvest. It is the first part of that first fruit (bunch) which is to be given to the lord. Let's say it another way; the portion which belongs to God would be the first part or the first ripened hand.

- Exodus 23:19; 34:26 and Deuteronomy 26:2, 10 reads "The first of the first fruit of thy land, etc. belong to God and should be brought to His house".

- Leviticus 2:12, 14 "If you offer a grain offering **of** first fruit…" *(Note that "of" here means a part of the whole).*

- Leviticus 23:9-11 the offering of the first fruit is a command offering N.B. it still says that what God wants is a part of the first harvest, not the whole harvest.

- Leviticus 23:17; Numbers 15:17-21 indicate that as we get blessed, we should bring a portion to God, e.g., in Biblical terms, whatever two-tenths ephah of flour can bake, two of these belong to God.

- The first fruit can be brought in on special occasions- (Numbers 28:26.)
- The first fruit is given for the Lord's work of feeding people (2Kings 4:42.)
- The first fruit is shown as a tithe of everything (2Chronicles 31:5.)
- The first fruit is shown as the first of all things - son, livestock, cattle, and fruit. It should be given to the Gate Keepers (Nehemiah 10:35-39; 12:44; 13:31.)
- A nation can be a type of first fruit (Jeremiah 2:2,3)
- Epaenetus is a type first fruit for his household to be saved (Romans 16:5.)
- The best of the first fruit is to be given to the priest as his own. He should then release a blessing to your house (Ezekiel 44:30.)

Stewardship over the tithes

The Purpose of the tithes: -

a) To pay those who serve in and around the Temple/Church (Numbers 18:2-24)
b) To be used to the care for the widows, orphans and the down-and-out of the faith- (Deuteronomy 26:12 – 15).
c) A portion should be used in a public feast at the (Temple) Church for the ones who carried it in and others (Deuteronomy 14:22-29).
d) To unlock the blessing of God in your life (Malachi 3:10).
e) To release God's rebuke against the seed eater/devourer (Malachi 3:11).
f) To prevent a curse from sticking to our lives. (Malachi 3:8-9).

g) To show the true posture of our heart (Matthew 6:19 – 21, 33).

h) To prove our faithfulness and obedience to God's Word (Deuteronomy 26:13 – 16).

Other scriptures on the principle of stewardship/giving

a) Those who deal with a slack hand will become poor (Proverbs 10:4).

b) The hand of the diligent will rule (Proverbs 10:4b; 12:24).

c) The slothful man does not roast what he catches (Proverbs 12:27).

d) The sluggard deserves and has nothing. (Proverbs 13:4, 11).

e) The one who scatters increases. (Genesis 8:22; Proverbs 11:24).

f) There is a reward for giving services/ laboring (Proverbs 14:23; 16:26; 14:4).

Mindsets that must be overcome as steward

a) He who observes the wind will not sow (Ecclesiastes 11:1-6)

b) Excuses people give as to why they can't overcome (Proverbs. 20:4; 22:13)

c) Slothfulness brings us to poverty (Proverbs. 13:23; 18:9)

d) Faith without works is dead standing alone (James 1:22-25; 2:14-26)

e) God will bless the work of our hands (Psalm 1:1-3)

9

Growing through Obedience

As Christians we are expected to be in submission to the Lordship of Jesus Christ and to walk in absolute obedience to Him.

> *"And He said to them all, if any man will come after Me, let him deny himself, and take up his cross daily, and follow Me. For whosoever will save his life shall lose it: but whosoever will lose his life for my sake, the same shall find it." - Luke 9: 23 - 24*

Obedience defined

(i) Obedience is the test of our love for God. (John 14: 15.)

(ii) If we acknowledge that Jesus is Lord, then He expects us to do what He says. (Luke 6: 46.)

(iii) When we build our lives in obedience to what God says then it is likened to a man building his house on a rock which, when challenged by the adversities of life, stands strong and unmovable – (Matthew 7:24 – 27.)

(iv) God expects us to be obedient to even the seemingly insignificant issues. (Matthew 5: 18 – 19.)

(v) Our faith must have corresponding obedient actions (works). (James 2:17.)

(vi) God puts disobedience and rebellion in the same category as idolatry and witchcraft and such actions can result in us being disqualified from the purposes of God for our lives – (1 Samuel 15:22 – 23.)

(vii) Obedience to God gives us the "spiritually legal" rights to use the spiritual weapons given to us in scripture against the enemy, effectively and successfully – (2Corinthians 10: 4-6.)

God is more interested in your act of obedience than your verbal commitment – (Matthew 21:28–31; Luke 6:46.)

Results of obedience

i.   You may be persecuted – (2 Timothy 3:12.)
ii. Answers to your prayers are guaranteed – (1 John. 3:22.)
iii. God will make our enemies to be at peace with us – (Proverbs 16:7.)
iv. Healing of our bodies – (Exodus 15:26.)
v.   Blessings in our lives – (Deuteronomy 28: 1 – 2.)
vi. Our success is guaranteed – (Joshua 1: 8.)
vii. Our children are blessed – (Deuteronomy 28: 4.)

Let us therefore endeavor to be obedient to the words of our Lord Jesus Christ.

10

Fellowship with the Saints

The Bible tells us that as Christians we are a family; we are brothers and sisters -Ephesians. 2:19 and 3:15 "Now therefore ye are no more strangers and foreigners, but fellow-citizens with the Saints and of the household of God… Of whom the whole family in heaven and earth is named."

We are also encouraged to assemble together and fellowship with each other. Hebrews 10:25 "Not forsaking the assembling of ourselves together as the manner of some is; but exhorting one another: and so much the more, as ye see the day approaching." Psalm 107:32 "Let them exalt him also in the congregation of the people and praise him in the assembly of the elders."

Unity must be our watchword

- Psalm 133:1 "Behold, how good and how pleasant it is for brethren to *dwell together in unity*."
- Ephesians 4:3 "Endeavoring to *keep the unity* of the Spirit in the bond of peace." (Matthew 5:23, 24.)
- As Christians, when we band ourselves together, we are guaranteed victory – (Leviticus 26:7 – 8 and Matthew 18:19 – 20.) We must love each other – (Romans 12:10; 1 Peter 1:22; John 13:35; John 15:13.)
- Love is the only real debt we should have for each other. (Romans 13:8)

- As we love each other we show that we are born and taught of God – (1John 4:7 -12; 1 Timothy 4:9)
- It is our love for each other that makes us weigh what we say to each other – (Ephesians 4:29; Colossian 4:6)
- We do not backbite each other or speak well of a person to their face and attack and malign them behind their back – (Psalm 15: 3.)
- We do not slander or to be a talebearer on each other – (Proverbs 18:8; 26:20.)
- It is because we love each other why we speak the truth in love – (Ephesians 4: 15-16)
- We must be willing to share with our brethren in natural and spiritual things – (Galatians 6: 2: Romans 12:15: 1 John 3: 17 – 18.)
- The early church is a good example of true sharing and fellowship – (Acts 4: 32– 35 1 Corinthians 16: 1-4)
- We are instructed how to relate to the brethren – (1 Timothy 5:1 – 2)

We are to treat: -

(i) Older men as fathers – not as outdated irritants, but with respect. (Leviticus 19: 23; Titus 2: 2)
(ii) Older women as mothers – not as outdated irritants, but with respect. (Titus 2:3-5)
(iii) Younger men as brothers – not as the competition or potential husbands or boyfriends.
(iv) Younger women as sisters – not as the competition or potential wives or girlfriends.

Because we are still being matured, there are times we may have an area that we may need help with. God expects us to turn to the brethren for help – (James 5:16; Galatians 6:1.)

In order to deal with brethren sinning against us or rifts in the relationship between us see – (Matthew 5:23-24; Luke17:3-4; Matthew 18:15 – 17.) Note that the issue of public disciplining of a Believer should be as a last resort after all else have failed. Also see (Proverbs 27:5; Ecclesiastics 7:5; 1 Timothy 5:20)

"Behold, how good and pleasant it is for brethren to dwell together in unity"! (Psalm 133:1)

11

The Future Fate of Mankind

The Scriptures are quite clear that the future of the righteous is different from that of the wicked.

Daniel 12 v 2: "And many of them that sleep in the dust of the earth shall awake, some to **everlasting life**, and some to **shame and everlasting contempt.**"

Matthew 25 v 31 – 46 "… come ye blessed of my Father, **inherit the kingdom prepared for you**… Depart from me, ye cursed, into **everlasting fire**, prepared for the devil and his angels…"

Luke 16 v 19 – 31 "…But Abraham said, Son, remember that thou in thy lifetime receiveth thy good things and likewise Lazarus evil things: but now **he is comforted, and thou art tormented…**"

A record of our actions is kept, and on that Day of Judgment God will use it to judge us. *(Jeremiah 17:1)* - "The **sin of Judah is written** with a pen of iron…" *(Malachi 3:16* - "Then they that feared the Lord spake often one to another: and the Lord hearkened, and heard it, **and a book of remembrance was written before Him for them that feared the Lord**, and that thought upon his name."

Revelation 20:12 - "And I saw the dead, small and great, stand before God; and the books were opened: and another book was opened, which is the book of life: and the dead were judged out of those things which were written in the books, according to their works."

Acts 7:60 - "And he kneeled down, and cried with a loud voice, Lord lay not this sin to their charge. And when he had said this, he fell asleep."

Future fate of the Righteous

(i)   We get honor from the King – (Luke12:37.)
(ii) We are glorified with the King – (Colossians 3:4.)
(iii) We shall receive a fadeless crown of glory – (1 Peter 5:4.)
(iv) We shall have no more sorrow – (Revelation 21:4.)
(v)   We shall have eternal fellowship with the Lord – (1 Thessalonians 4:17.)

Obedience is the condition for entry into the rewards of God – (Revelation 22:14.)

Future fate of the wicked

(i)   They shall be given over by God – (Romans 1:24 – 28.)
(ii) They will be deceived by the Antichrist – (2 Thessalonians 2:10 – 11.)
(iii) They will experience God's wrath during the tribulation – (Revelation 9:3 – 6.)

(iv) They will be banished from God – (Matthew 7:23; Matthew 22:13.)

(v) Their end will be everlasting fire – (Matthew 25:41; Revelation 21:8.)

(vi) They shall be tormented by worms – (Mark 9:48.)

Repentance will ensure that a person escapes God's judgment – (Ezekiel 33:14–16.)

12

The Ministry of Reconciliation

God expects us to be actively involved in reconciling men back to Him.

> *As Believers we have been given the ministry of reconciliation, and God has committed to us the word of reconciliation.* – *(2 Corinthians 5:18-19)*

Jesus commands His church to preach the gospel to every creature Mark 16:15 and to disciple (teach) the nations or ethnos, (Gr.): - race, tribe, language and sub culture. (Matthew 28:19.)

The basic gospel message

(i) All men have sinned against God.
- Psalm 51:5: - "I was born in sin and shaped in iniquity"
- Romans 3:10: - "…There is none righteous, no, not one."
- Romans 3:23: - "For all have sinned and come short of the glory of God."

(ii) When man sinned, he placed himself under the penalty of sin: -
- Genesis 2:17: - "…in the day that you eat thereof thou shall surely die"
- Ezekiel 18:20: - "The soul that sins, it shall die…"
- Deuteronomy 28:15 - 68 – they speak of the consequences (curses) for disobedience.

- Psalm 9:17: - "The wicked shall be turned into hell, and all the nations that forget God."

Penalties of sin

- Death – (Ezekiel 18:20)
- Sickness – (Exodus 13:26)
- Poverty – (Proverbs 6:9-11; 2 Timothy 3:10)
- Abuse – (1 Corinthians 6:9)
- Bondage – (Matthew 4:24; Acts 16:16; 2 Timothy 2:26)
- Failure – (Matthew 25:18; 24-26)
- Oppression – (Mark 7:26; Matthew 8:16)
- Eternal separation from God and torture – (Matthew 25:41; Revelation 21:8)

Jesus – The sacrifice that paid the price for sin

(i) Jesus died on the cross for the sins of mankind (He took the penalty of sin for mankind), was buried, rose from the dead and ascended to the Father where he sits at His right hand making intercession (petition) for us.

- Romans 5:8: - "…while we were yet sinners, Christ died for us."
- Romans 14:9: - "For to this end Christ both died, and rose, and revived, that he might be Lord both of the dead and living"
- Hebrews 7:25: - "…he ever lives to make intercession for them."

(ii) Jesus is the only one appointed by God whereby a man can gain access to God and His salvation.

- Acts 4:12: - "Neither is there salvation in any other: for there is none other name under heaven given among men, whereby we must be saved."

- John 14:6: - "Jesus said unto them, I am the Way, the Truth, and the Life: no man cometh unto the Father, but by me."

(iii) All the good works are not good enough to save us from the penalty of sin and put us in right standing with God.

- Ephesians 2:8 – 9: - "For by grace are ye saved through faith; and that not of yourselves: it is the gift of God: not of works, lest any man should boast." -Acts 10:1 – 6.

(iv) When we receive Jesus as Lord over our lives He forgives us and saves us from the power and penalty of sin.

- Psalm 103:3 – 6
- Romans 6:11 – 14
- Galatians 3:13: - "Christ hath redeemed us from the curse of the law, being made a curse for us: for it is written, cursed is every one that hangs on a tree."

How to Reconcile a Person to God

- John 1:12; Romans 10: 9-10
- Encourage them to repent or turn from a life sin and living without God.
- They must Believe/recognize that Jesus is raised from the dead and is reigning at the right hand of God the Father. (1Corintians 15:25; Hebrew 1:13)
- With their mouth confess/acknowledge and declare Him to be Lord over their lives.

What happens to the person that accepts Jesus as Lord?

2 Corinthians 5:17: - "Therefore if any man be in Christ, he is a new creature: old things are passed away; behold all things are become new."

- He is born again (John 3:3,7)

- He is born of an incorruptible seed (1Peter 1:23)

What does Jesus expect from us as Believers?

- To live above the power of sin (that is) to live in holiness – (Romans 6:1-2; Psalm 119:9.)
- To not willfully commit sin (1John 3:8; Hebrews 10:26-31)
- To live above the penalty of sin – (Romans 5:17 & 18.)
- To live in fellowship with God means to always pray and to read the Word – (Ephesians 6:18; Psalm 119:11).
- To live in relationship and harmony with other Believers (Church attendance and involvement included) – (Hebrews 10:25; Ephesians 4:3,16).
- To share the gospel with those around us (Matthew 28:19-20.)
- To make disciples of others (Matthew 28:19.)
- To commit our lives (who we are and what we possess) to building His Kingdom – (Deuteronomy 8:18; Acts 4:34-35.)

Sharing The Gospel (your faith)

The gospel is the birth/coming, death, burial, bodily resurrection, second coming of the Lord Jesus Christ and his kingdom – (John. 3:16; 1 Corinthians 15:1-6)

(v) Always be prepared (in prayer and word). (2 Timothy 2:15; 1 Peter 3:15)

(vi) Declare the Lordship of Jesus over the situation/circumstance you are going to approach. (2 Corinthians 3:5,6; 4:7)

(vii) Begin where people's interests are and guide the conversation towards Jesus. (Acts 8:27 -35)

(viii) Always bring them to a place of decision. (2 Corinthians 5:11)

(ix) Expect God to confirm His word with signs and to convict persons. (Mark 16:20.)

(x) Expect people to respond to the Gospel. (Psalm 106:6): - "He that goes forth and weeping, bearing precious seed shall doubtless come again with rejoicing, bringing his sheaves with him."

(xi) Luke 10:2: - "…the harvest truly is great, but the laborers are few: pray ye therefore the Lord of the harvest that he would send forth laborers into His harvest".

An example to remember

This is an example of a conversation you could have with someone with who you are sharing the Gospel. You would need to have time to show them the Scriptures.

"Good day (Mr. Mrs. Miss.) Mr. Jones, this is a lovely day isn't it? It is a day in which Christ could come again. Did you know that the Bible Says?

1) *All men are sinners, and need to be saved*
   - Romans 3 vs. 10-12, 23 says "…As it is written, there is none righteous, no, not one: there is none that understandeth, there is none that seeketh after God. They are all gone out of the way, they are together become unprofitable; there is none that doeth good, no, not one."
   - "…For all have sinned, and come short of the Glory of God;"
   - Jeremiah 17 v 9 "…The heart is deceitful above all things, and desperately wicked: who can know it?"
   - And that in order to have a new life The Bible tells us "…Jesus answered and said unto him, 'verily, verily, I say unto thee, except a man be born again, he cannot see the Kingdom of God". (John 3:3.)

How can we be born again?

By recognizing that:

2) *Jesus is God's Answer and the only Way to be saved*
- Jesus tells us in *John 14 v 6*, "I am the way, the truth, and the life: no man cometh unto the Father, but by me
- The Bible went on to say in *Acts 4 v 12* "…Neither is there salvation in any other: for there is none other name under heaven given among men, whereby we must be saved." And *I Timothy 1 v 15* "…this is a faithful saying, and worthy of all acceptation, that Christ Jesus came into the world to save sinners, of whom I am chief."

Just how did Jesus make this provision?

3) *By dying on a cross for our sins.*
The Bible tells us so in the following passages:

- I Corinthians 15 v 3-4 "…for I delivered unto you first of all that which I also received, how that Christ died for our sins according to the scripture; and that He was buried, and that he rose again the third day according to the Scriptures."
- I Peter 2 v 24 "…who his own self bare our sins in His own body on the tree that we, being dead to sins, should live unto righteousness: by whose stripes ye were healed."
- Romans 4 v 25 "…who was delivered for our offences and was raised again for our justification."

How do we make use of this provision?

We need to seek and have a personal relationship experience with Jesus. Here is what the Bible has to say about this:

- John 1:12 "…but as many as received Him, to them gave He power to become the sons of God, even to them that believed on His name:"
- Romans 10:9-10 "…that if thou shalt confess with thy mouth the Lord Jesus, and shalt believe in your heart that God hath raised Him from the dead, thou shalt be saved. For with the heart man believeth unto righteousness; and with the mouth confession is made unto salvation."
- Acts 2:38 "…then Peter said unto them, Repent, and be baptized every one of you in the name of Jesus Christ for the remission of sins, and ye shall receive the gift of the Holy Ghost."
- Acts 16:31 "…and they said, "Believe on the Lord Jesus Christ, and thou shalt be saved, and thy house.""

Now that you have seen your need for a new life, won't you make the following steps to receiving Christ: -

Repent of (or turn from) your sinful ways. (Mark 1:15; Luke13:5; Acts 3; 19)

(i) Believe the Gospel. (1 Timothy 1:15; Ephesians 2:8.)

(ii) Receive (ask) Jesus into your life. (John 1:12.)

(iii) Confess His Lordship over your life. (Romans10:10.)

(iv) Will you pray this prayer with me? -

Father, I confess that I have sinned and lived in rebellion against you and am worthy of your judgment. Jesus, you, however paid the penalty for my sins by dying on the cross and therefore I do not need to suffer the judgment for sin. I believe that you rose from the dead and are now reigning at God's right hand, and ask you

*to forgive my sins, cancel my past, come into my life and
be Lord of my life. Amen.*

13

God's Standard of Morality

What? know ye not that your body is the temple of the Holy Ghost which is in you, which ye have of God, and ye are not your own? (1Corinthians 6:9)

Morals have to do with standards of behavior and principles of right and wrong. God has established His standards as absolutes for the quality of life that He wanted man to live. However, due to man's love for sin, man has always sought for an alternative way which is the opposite of what God has set as His standard.

Man's standards of morality then are best described in these three scriptures, Man is described to be (1) "lovers pleasure more than lovers of God" (2) "The Lord saw... that every intention of the thoughts of his heart was only evil continually" and (3) "The heart is deceitful above all things, and desperately sick (wicked KJV); who can understand it?" (2Timothy 3:2-7; Genesis 6:5; Jeremiah 17:9, 10) ESV.

In the area of human sexuality God set out His ideal plan for man's sexual behavior both publicly and privately. These are set out in this Word as absolute (unchangeable) truths/principles based on His love for and foreknowledge of His creation. The time may change, the structure of the nation may change but God's Word remains forever (Isaiah 55:7-11)

We believe that The Word of God has the final say about morality and immorality, human sexuality; that sexual intercourse in humans is reserved for Biblical marriage of one man to one woman joined in Holy matrimony. "They two became one flesh". (Genesis 2:21-25; Ephesians 5:31)

Homosexuality /Sodomy

God has made very clear His position on the matter of homosexuality: it is an abnormal, ungodly, debasing, abominable act. He commands that this should not be practiced by neither male nor female, and under Levitical law it would be punishable by death. (Leviticus 20:13). It must be greatly emphasized that contrary to what some of our modern-day Popes, Priests, Bishops, Apostles, Prophets, Evangelists, Teachers, Pastors, Elders, Deacons, Governments or any other category of institution may tell you, (Jeremiah 23:11-20) ESV. God's mind on this matter has not changed; but His **provision** for remedy has more hope, mercy and grace to it. Governments may pass laws to make the practice legal as well as to bar persons from speaking out about the truth of Sodomy/ homosexuality, but no government, no military, no police force, will be able to stop God when He decides to pour out His judgment against this sin. In fact, the governments themselves, will be judged for their complicit behavior (Psalm 9:17-20) ESV. In His desire to extend his mercy and to have "all people to be saved and to come to the knowledge of the truth" (1Timothy 2:4) ESV. He has sent his Son Jesus the Christ for the **deliverance / freedom and cure** for **anyone** who will truly want help and will surrender and cry out to him.

Jesus said "The Spirit of the Lord is upon me, because He has anointed me to proclaim good news to the poor. He has sent me to proclaim liberty to the captives and recovering of sight to the blind, to set at liberty those who are oppressed, to proclaim the year of the Lord's favor."   (Luke 4:18, 19; Isaiah 61:1-4) ESV.

John said of Jesus "For God so loved the world, that He gave His only Son, that whoever believes in Him should not perish but have eternal life. For God did not send His Son into the world to condemn the world, but in order that the world might be saved through Him. (John 3:16, 17) ESV.

Paul confirms this in the book Corinthians "Or do you not know that the unrighteous will not inherit the Kingdom of God? Do not be deceived: neither the sexually immoral, nor idolaters, nor adulterers, nor men who practice homosexuality, nor thieves, nor the greedy, nor drunkards, nor revilers, nor swindlers will inherit the Kingdom of God. And such were some of you. But you were washed, you were sanctified, you were justified in the name of the Lord Jesus Christ and by the Spirit of our God". (1Corintians 6:9-11) ESV.

Paul went on to say "Who (God) will have all men to be saved, and to come unto the knowledge of the truth. For there is one God, and one Mediator between God and men, the man Christ Jesus; who gave himself a ransom for all, to be testified in due time". (1Timothy 2:4-6)

God's reason for hating and Judging Sodomy

The judgment comes only to those who have rejected Him, Christ Jesus, as the provision /cure (Romans 1:24-31). Note verse 32: "Though they know God's righteous decree that those who practice such things deserve to die, they not only do them but give approval to those who practice them". ESV.

The Lord will judge presumptuous sin (Hebrews 10: 26-31). Note, in verse 30 it clearly says "The Lord will judge his people".

The judgment of God did not only fall on Sodom and Gomorrah but upon all the cities that bought into and practiced their sin. Jude said this "Just as Sodom and Gomorrah and the surrounding cities, which likewise indulged in sexual immorality and pursued unnatural desire, serve as an example by undergoing a punishment of eternal fire. Yet in like manner these people also, relying on their dreams, defile the flesh, reject authority, and blaspheme the glorious ones". (Jeremiah 50:40; Jude 1:7, 8)

Jesus, using John the Baptizer as an example and speaking against the Romans and their immorality, especially homosexuality, said this, "**John was not effeminate**". "What then did you go out to see? A man dressed in soft (: - effeminate) clothing? Behold, those who wear soft clothing are in kings' houses" (Matthew 11:8). By extension he is saying **the ones I have called** to prepare the way for my coming / second coming, **the ones upon whom I have rest the spirit of Elijah, my prophets, are not homosexual / man sodomizing man**. (MSM)

A few special points to note on the matter:

(1) <u>The practitioners of Sodomy know it is wrong</u>

Using the book entitled *"After the Ball: How America Will Conquer its Fear and Hatred of Gays in the 90's"* (Plume book, 1989, ISBN: 0452264987) by Marshall Kirk a psychologist (now deceased), from Harvard University, and Dr. Hunter Madsen who was an expert in public persuasion tactics and Public Relations Specialist, **Focus on the Family** set out the six-points Agenda of the homosexual community, in order to fulfill their goal.

➢ Talk about gays and gayness as loudly as often as possible;

- ➢ Portray gays as victims and not as aggressive terrorists;
- ➢ Give homosexual protectors a just cause; (legal status)
- ➢ Make gays look good;
- ➢ Make the victimizers look bad;
- ➢ Get funds from corporate America

The authors also reveal in the book their knowledge /insight of what they know to be right and wrong, what is sinful and what is holy and God's verdict on the practice.

> *"There can be no doubt that Christianity represents the greatest obstacle to the normalization of homosexual behavior. It cannot be otherwise because of the **clear biblical teachings** concerning the **inherent sinfulness of homosexuality in all forms** and the **normality of heterosexual marriage"**.*

Again, the scripture said "Though they know God's righteous decree that those who practice such things deserve to die, they not only do them but give approval to those who practice them" (Romans 1:32) ESV.

NB: These six-point strategies were first published in Guide Magazine, a homosexual publication, in November 1987 in an article entitled **"The Overhauling of Straight America"** and was written by Marshall K. Kirk and Erastes Pill. The above-mentioned book was only an expansion on those strategies.

(http://library.gayhomeland.org/0018/EN/EN_Overhauling_Straight.htm)

(2) Sodomy was one of the diabolic tools of slavery design to mar the image of God in man

It must be highlighted that through the slavery that had been perpetrated upon the Africans that were abducted and sold to the nations of the world and their colonies. In the Caribbean; a great deal of these men was sodomized on these ships to satisfy the insatiable perverse appetites of their captors.

There was also an horrendous practice that was done particularly in Jamaica; the slave masters establish what was called seasoning farms, on which these European slave masters, as a means of breaking, subduing and subjecting strong black slave men deemed rebellious, would publicly sodomize them in the presence of their entire family – wives, children and entire slave population on their plantations, under an act that was called **"Buck Breaking or Buck Busting"**. (https://youtu.be/3EsqvGX48zE?t=41)

This violation was both humiliating and emasculating. Homosexuality was a diabolic tool used by our Colonial slave-masters to weaken men, and to bring them into subjection instead of building their manhood and the image of God that they represent.

(3) Sodomy was introduced in the earth by fallen angels

To say Sodomy/ homosexuality is diabolic, is to bring clarity to Paul discourse/ arguments in Romans Chapter one in which he not only addresses the practice of his day but he sought to show how this sinful practice started to begin with. Drawing his knowledge of Genesis and the

Pseudepigraphal book, "The Book of Enoch" (which was popularly known in their time) he established the source problem as the shift from Creator worship to creature worship.

This had not begun at the time of writing of the book of Romans but rather with the angels (ben Elohiym / Eloheem) "sons of God" which came and entered into sexual relationship with the earthly woman (daughters of men) and produced Nephilim / giants (Genesis 6: 1-7) in corroborating the Genesis chapter six account; The Book Of Enoch tells us that after the initial sin and subsequent casting down of Satan and one third of the angels another; two hundred more angels lead by one called Semjâzâ /Sêmîazâz came and they were the ones that had sexual relations with the women and produced the Nephilim / giants. Enoch went on to name twenty of them and tells what they practiced and taught and how that impacted on the inhabitant of the world. (Enoch 6:1-8). In chapter eight of the Book of Enoch (a Pseudepigrapha) we read;

> *"And Azâzêl taught men to make swords, and knives, and shields, and breastplates, and made known to them the metals of the earth and the art of working them, and bracelets, and ornaments, and the use of antimony, and the beautifying of the eyelids, and all kinds of costly stones, and all colouring tinctures. 2.* ***And there arose much godlessness, and they committed fornication,*** *and they were led astray, and became corrupt in all their ways. Semjâzâ taught enchantments, and root-cuttings, Armârôs the*

76

resolving of enchantments, Barâqîjâl, (taught) astrology, Kôkabêl the constellations, Ezêqêêl the knowledge of the clouds, Araqiêl the signs of the earth, Shamsiêl the signs of the sun and Sariêl the course of the moon. And as men perished, they cried, and their cry went up to heaven . . ." (http://www.sacred-texts.com/bib/boe/boe009.htm)

It must be noted that while Adam's sin and fall brought sin into the world and because of this breach we are all born with sin, it is the invasion of the fallen angels that took man to a whole new level of decadence and rejection of God /YHVH. In the end God/YHVH judge the whole world with a flood. Jesus in peaking to the crowds warns of the pending end time judgment by drawing a parallel between then and His day with a prophetic foreshadowing of our day, when He said;

"Just as it was in the days of Noah, so will it be in the days of the Son of Man. They were eating and drinking and marrying and being given in marriage, until the day when Noah entered the ark, and the flood came and destroyed them all". (Luke 17:2527) He also continued by saying;

"Likewise, just as it was in the days of Lot—they were eating and drinking, buying and selling, planting and building, but on the day when Lot went out from Sodom, fire and sulfur rained from heaven and destroyed them all, so will it be on the day when the Son of Man is revealed". (Luke 17:28-30).

The things that characterizes these times were the wantonness and unnatural sexual indulgence along with the other excesses and lack of regard for and/or the replacement God. Jesus in wanting to rekindle the fear of God in them and us, charges us,

"Remember Lot's wife". (Luke 17:32

Adultery and fornication

In a generation where we are being taught that one should be free to love / have sex with whomever and with whatever they choose, the Word of God stands as bedrock, a sure place where the truth can be found on these subjects. It gives us insight on the harmful results of the breach of any system that God has established in the earth and these subjects are no exception.

- The body is not made for fornication (1Corinthions 6:13)
- We are advised to run from or flee fornication (1 Corinthians 6:18; 7:2; Colossian 3:5)
- It is the will of God that we abstain from fornication (1 Timothy 4:3)
- God have judged fornication in the past and will do it again (1 Corinthians 10:8; Jude 1:7)
- A man or woman should find all their satisfaction in the spouse they marry. (Proverbs 5:15-20)
- God holds the partner who breaches the marriage responsible. (Proverbs.5:23; 6:24-29),
- Adultery releases the curse of poverty in one's marriage (Proverbs 6:26)
- Adultery releases sickness to affect one's home (Proverbs 5:9b, 11)
- Adultery destroys one's integrity and honour (Proverbs 5:9)
- Adultery causes deep and painful regrets (Proverbs 5:12-13, 22)
- Adultery is caused by greed and lust (Exodus 20:17)

78

- In Job the oldest book in the Bible, Job said, "...If I have committed adultery with another man's wife, then let someone take my wife and sleep with her" (Job 31:9-11).
- God said adulterers and whoremongers shall have their part in hell (1 Corinthians 6:9.)
- In Revelation Jesus said of some of the Churches "...you have allowed that woman Jezebel (spirit) to teach, causing my people to commit fornication". This spirit was found in leadership (Rev. 2: 20 -23.)
- Paul writes "...but fornicators and adulterers God will judge". (Hebrews 13:4)
- Paul then said. "Whomever defiles the temple of God, him will God destroy" (2 Corinthians 3:17.)

Incest

In our country Jamaica incest is against the law therefore all acts of incest should be reported to the Police, especially those of father to his daughter or step-father to step-daughter. Let the law of the land run its course. Incest is not just an attack on Biblical morality, but an attack on the family and its posterity.

Leviticus 18:1 -26; 20:9-21 speaks on the matter of sexual intercourse between family members, and God forbids this in every form, whether it is:

- Father and daughter
- Mother and son
- Father and step-daughter
- Mother and step-son
- Brother and sister
- Son and step-mother
- Son and aunt

- Cousin and cousin

Bestiality or Zoophilia

I was of the opinion that the practice of Bestiality was a thing of the past or not commonly practiced in our days, but I was rudely awakened by an article printed in "The Outlook" A magazine section of the Jamaica Sunday Gleaner, dated November 12, 2006, entitled **"Sex with Animals"** written by *Dr. Heather Little-White (now deceased)*. In this article, it was stated that a man died from internal injuries he received after having sex with a stallion. This was said to have happen at a ranch used by a bestiality ring in the North Western United States.

The article went on to say that bestiality is legal in some states of the United States and that a number of small animals such as dogs, cats and chickens have died from these human-to-animal sexual contacts.

The Scriptures however stand guard against this practice for the protection of morality and the family. (Leviticus 18:23; 20:15.) The scripture also shows that these practices will disqualifies a person from spending eternity with Christ. Therefore, the father offers His son Jesus and His blood as His deliverance His cure. (1 Corinthians 6:9-11; 1 John 1:5-10) ESV

NB. It should be understood that the USA position on bestiality remains same to this day, "This table details state laws prohibiting sexual conduct between humans and animals. Most states (about 45) have some provision that criminalizes engaging in sexual conduct with animals. Hawaii, Kentucky, New Mexico, West Virginia and Wyoming, as well as the District of Columbia, do not have laws addressing this conduct."

Published by Rebecca F Wisch in 2017 for the Michigan State University College of Law Primary Citation: Animal Legal & Historical Center. (https://www.animallaw.info/topic/table-state-animal-sexual-assault-laws)

Sexual relation with animals are further spoken of in the scripture in the following ways

    i.   It is a curse to have sexual relation with an animal (Deuteronomy 27:21)

    ii.   A punishment was always attach to Bestiality, the Old Testament recommend the killing of both the human and the animal. (Exodus 22:19; Leviticus 20:15,16) I believe it should be a criminal offence and the person should go through psychiatric evaluation and deliverance.

    iii.   Bestiality is a perversion and a land polluting immoral sin, that ultimately will attract God's judgments and lands he has bless us with. (Leviticus 18:23-30)

14

Biblical Morality and Church Leadership

I thought I had finished writing this book, when the Lord spoke to me about addressing morality, or the lack thereof, in Church leadership, and to explain the Biblical recourse laid out for the victims of an immoral Church leader, and the responsibility of others in leadership to stop such abuse of power.

It must be understood that the Church is not exempt from acts of immorality. Whether it is the so-called 'coming out of the closet' of those involved in the shameful act of homosexuality, or the disgraceful exposure of those that molest small children (girls or boys) and teenagers in their care, or those who have an extra-marital relationship with a female member of their congregation, and upon discovery of a pregnancy, order an abortion and pay for it to be done in order to cover their tracks. The Church has had its fair share of the leaders who abuse their position of power and authority given to them to lead. The Apostle Paul said "...some things are too shameful to even mention". (Ephesians 5:12.)

The Bible has given clear-cut actions that should be brought to bear on the acts of sin and indiscretion done by leaders. These are both preventative and curative.

Preventative Guidelines

These guidelines speak to the leaders of being people of character

a) A Priest should be the husband of one wife (1 Timothy 3:2; Titus 1:6)

b) He should not be a wife beater or a striker (1 Timothy 3:3)

c) He should not be of the sort that creeps into houses and seduce silly women laden with sin (2 Timothy 3:6; 2 Timothy 2: 2.)

d) He should be proven - "...gold tried in the fire" (Revelation 3: 18)

e) He should walk worthy of the vocation to which he is called (1Timothy 6:1; Ephesians 4:1.)

f) Job said "I have made a covenant with my eyes "not to look at woman married or unmarried and lust" (Job 33:1.)

g) The fear of the Lord should rule our lives (1Corinthians 6:15 - 20; Proverbs 8:13)

h) Solomon counsels "Drink waters out of your own cistern and running waters out of your own well. Let thy fountains be dispersed abroad, and rivers of waters in the streets. Let them be only your own, and not strangers with thee. Let thy fountain be blessed: and rejoice with the wife of thy youth. Let her be as the loving hind and pleasant roe; let her breasts satisfy thee at all times; and be thou ravished always with her love. And why wilt thou, my son, be ravished with the love of a strange/adulterous woman, and embrace the bosom of a stranger? For the ways of a man are before the eyes of the LORD, and He ponders all his ways". (Proverbs 5: 15 -21)

Curative Guidelines

a. David said that ways (habits, character) can be cleansed (Psalm 119:9.)

b. Solomon said those who commit adultery lack understanding (Proverbs 6:32)

c. Paul said, "...flee youthful lust" (1 Corinthians 6: 18; 2 Timothy 2:22.)

d. God said in Deuteronomy 17:17 that "...a leader/king should not have many wives". (Deuteronomy 17:14-20)

e. Paul said such persons can be cured (1 Corinthians 6:9 - 11) God voices His judgment on fornicators /the Immoral

f. In Exodus 20 the Lord teaches us that there are penalties for sins that not only affect us but our children as well. "Thou shall not bow down thyself to them, nor serve them: for I the LORD thy God am a jealous God, visiting the iniquity of the fathers upon the children unto the third and fourth generation of them that hate me." (Exodus 20:5)

g. God then commanded "Thou shall not commit adultery (Exodus 20:14) and we should not "...covet our neighbor's wife" (Exodus 20:17.)

h. In Job the oldest book in the Bible, Job said, "...If I have committed adultery with another man's wife, then let someone take my wife and sleep with her" (Job 31:9-11.)

i. God said adulterers and whoremongers shall have their part in hell (1 Corinthians 6:9.)

j. In Revelation Jesus said of some of the Churches "...you have allowed that woman Jezebel (spirit) to teach, causing my people to commit fornication". This spirit was found in leadership (Rev. 2: 20 -23.)

k. The Bible says "…but fornicators and adulterers God will judge". (Hebrews13:4)

l. Paul then said. "Whomever defiles the temple of God, him will God destroy" (2 Corinthians 3:17.)

Examples of God's judgment on a leader (David)

For his fornication and immorality

David's sinful actions	Scripture Reference	Judgment that God pronounced or the curse released as a result of the sin(s)	Scripture reference	Judgment fulfilled	Scripture reference
David entertains lust	2 Samuel 11:2-8 2 Samuel 12:4	Amnon (David's son) lusts after Tamar (David's daughter) Absalom lusts for power	2 Samuel 13: 1-2 2 Samuel 15: 1-6	Absalom lusts for power	2 Samuel 15:1-6
David took /seized Uriah's wife *(ewe lamb)	2 Samuel 11:4 2 Samuel 12:4	Amnon seizes his sister (Tamar)	2 Samuel 13:11	Absalom seizes the throne	2 Samuel 15:10-17
David did two acts of evil – adultery and murder	2 Samuel 11:3; 4 2 Samuel 12:9	God said to David "evil shall not leave your house" Absalom murdered his brother Amnon	2 Samuel 12:10-11 2 Samuel 13:28-29	Amnon did the evil of rape Absalom did the evil of defiling David's bed	2 Samuel 13:14-17 2 Samuel 16:22
David's sin began on the house top	2 Samuel 11:2	God said his wives would be violated on the same house top	2 Samuel 12:11	Absalom sleeps with ten of David's wives on the house top	2 Samuel 16:21-22

85

David's sinful actions	Scripture Reference	Judgment that God pronounced or the curse released as a result of the sin(s)	Scripture reference	Judgment fulfilled	Scripture reference
David's sin was adultery	2 Samuel 11:2-4	God said adultery will now be done against him	2 Samuel 12:11	Absalom committed adultery with David's 10 wives	2 Samuel 16:22
David plotted and conspired for the death of Uriah	2 Samuel 11:14-17	Absalom plots and conspires for the death of David, and for his throne	2 Samuel 15:1-6	Absalom plots and conspires for Amnon's death	2 Samuel 13:22-29
David killed Uriah by the sword of the Ammonites (son of incest)	Genesis 19;31-38 / 2 Samuel 12:9	Incest was released into his house	2 Samuel 12:11-12	Amnon raped his half-sister, Absalom (David's son) slept with his wives	2 Samuel 13:14, 20 / 2 Samuel 16:20-22
David did his sin under the cover of dusk	2 Samuel 12:12	God said this act will be done in brightness of day	2 Samuel 12:12	Absalom slept with David's wives at noon / Absalom was killed at noon	2 Samuel 16:22 / 2 Samuel 18:14
David's sin was an act of despising and showing disrespect to God's leadership	2 Samuel 12:7-9	Despise and disrespect was released against his leadership	2 Samuel 12:7-9	Absalom stole the heart of the people	2 Samuel 15:6
David's sin destroyed the house of	2 Samuel 11:26	His house and the flame of his heart was put	2 Samuel 18:9-15	Absalom the most beautiful"	2 Samuel 18:14

David's sinful actions	Scripture Reference	Judgment that God pronounced or the curse released as a result of the sin(s)	Scripture reference	Judgment fulfilled	Scripture reference
Uriah :- (Flame of God)		out (Absalom – father of peace)		was killed by Joab	

Please note. God's judgment on David for his sin of adultery with Bathsheba started with the death of the child and ended with the death of Absalom. (2 Samuel 12; 10-15; 2 Samuel 13:14-17; 2 Samuel 18:16-17.)

Examples of *God judgment on Irresponsible leadership*

There is a lie that the enemy has sown in Christ's Church, especially the Charismatic and Pentecostal Bible-believing churches, which is, if someone knows that a leader, especially an Apostle, Prophet, Pastor, Teacher or Evangelist is involved in immorality (sin), they should not say this to someone else in leadership, or they should not confront them because if they do then they would have **"touched the Lord's Anointed"**. So, they resort to just praying about the matter. Just look at what God did to Eli for his refusal to take action.

Examples of God judging irresponsible leadership

(The House of Eli) in the Old Testament

Sins of Eli	Scripture Reference	Judgment God pronounced or curse released as a result of the sin(s)	Scripture Reference	Judgment fulfilled	Scripture Reference
Disrespectful to God; Idolatry	1 Samuel 2:29 1 Samuel 2:30b	Lightly esteemed (to bring into a curse) A curse of rejection and poverty	1 Samuel 2:30 1 Samuel 2:36	God starts speaking to Samuel and not Eli Abiathar (Father of Abundance) is now sent to work the field	1 Samuel 3:10-15 1 Kings 2:26
Taking God for granted/kick at or trample on God's sacrifices	1 Samuel 2:29	This sin shall not be pardoned forever; God shall become his enemy He struck the House of Israel	1 Samuel 3:13 1 Samuel 2:32 1 Samuel 3:11-12	Eli died not forgiven; His daughter-in-law died in childbirth	1 Samuel 4:13-18 1 Samuel 4:18-20
Spiritual Shortsightedness blind	1 Samuel 3:2	His two sons would die in one day as a sign God's glory would depart	1 Samuel 2:34 1 Samuel 3:11,12	Sons died Glory departed (the word used to describe this is Ichabod)	1 Samuel 4:11 1 Samuel 4:9-10
Presumptuous	1 Samuel 3:13	God will make a final end of Eli's house	1 Samuel 3:12	Abiathar stripped	1 Kings 2:26-27
Loss of the fear of God	1 Samuel 2:22	God would not fight for nor defend them	1 Samuel 4;9, 10	God did not help them	1 Samuel 4:9-10

Sins of Eli	Scripture Reference	Judgment God pronounced or curse released as a result of the sin(s)	Scripture Reference	Judgment fulfilled	Scripture Reference
Irresponsible and condoning	1 Samuel 2:22-25 1 Samuel 3:13b	I will cut off your (arm, authority / shoulder) There shall not be an old man in your house	1 Samuel 2:31-33 1 Samuel 2:31	Hophni & Phinehas (Eli's sons) killed Saul as king killed 85 priests one stone in one day	1 Samuel 4:11 1 Samuel 22:11-23

*Please note.

1) Only the tribe of Levi was named as the Priestly tribe (1 Samuel 2 :35; 3:11, 12.;1 Kings 2:27)

2) that the Priesthood did not shift from the tribe of Levi straight away but went to the older line of Aaron's sons. (of which is Zadok) (1 Chronicle 6:7,8; 9:11)

3) The absolute switch or total fulfillment of this prophecy of a moving of the priesthood from Levi to the tribe of Judah was fulfilled in Jesus. (Psalm 110:4; Hebrew 7:13, 14)

Some people may say we are under Grace and that God will not do this. They need to consider the following scriptures: (Ecclesiastes 10:8) God is not mocked (Galatians 6:7-8); Hebrews 10:26-31 (God's response to presumptuous sin) – The Lord chastened. (Hebrews 12:5-11.)

Sins of Eli's sons and actions that should have been
Taken by Eli (the authority)

Sins of Eli's sons	Scripture Reference
Belial (to be a drunkard; homosexuality; sexual promiscuity; abusive (beat wives or treat their wives badly; to be filled with greed; liars; takers of bribe)	1 Samuel 2:12
Not knowing the Lord.	1 Samuel 2:12
They love to beat the system	1 Samuel 2:13-16
Violent, adulterous	1 Samuel 2: 15-16
	1 Samuel 2:22
Lustful, manipulative	1 Samuel 2:15-17
	1 Samuel 2: 22
Disrespectful of Father, abhor/scorn God and the dedicated things of God	1 Samuel 2:25b
	1 Samuel 21:17
Heartless/Presumptuous	1 Samuel 4:4
Lost the Fear of the Lord	1 Samuel 2:17; 29; 44
Vile	1 Samuel 3:13

As was shown in the first example (which refers to David's sins), the sin of immorality brings not only the judgment of God to one's life, but the wrath of God or the curse that God has declared against such sins (1 Samuel 2:6-10). Therefore, this table only shows the sins of the sons Eli, but the resulting judgment and wrath of God was meted out on (a) the father Eli, who should have exercised his authority over his sons; and (b) the entire household.

Old Testament laws that Eli should have observed to deal with the sins of his sons

- *Adultery:* Stoned to death
- ***Sins against their Office as Priests***: put out of the Priesthood.
- ***Corruption of bribery***: discharged from their public office as Judge.
- ***For the loss of the Fear of the Lord***: the curse of God's judgment should be spoken over them – that the Glory of the Lord would destroy them.

God judged the house of Eli for the sins of Hophni and Phinehas (his sons); and note that God did not stop at the two sons, but Eli himself and the generations after him were judged also. (1 Samuel 2:27-36; 1 Samuel 4:11, 17, And 18.)

A word of advice

Let me make something clear. If you knew that someone in leadership is actively involved in immorality, and did not say something to others in leadership, this makes you an accessory/accomplice to the crime (sin), or what the Bible calls partaker to another man's sin. (1Timothy 5:22)

1) The phrase "Touch not the Lord's Anointed" does not mean or refer to only those in leadership/Apostle Prophets, Pastors etc., upon whom hands was laid setting them apart for ministry, it was God's announcement to the surrounding nations, enemies of his people; to not trouble, harass, hurt, or attack his entire community of Believers (Israel then, the Church now) - His people as a whole, are His Anointed ones collectively. (1 Chronicles 16:16-23; Psalms 105:11-17)

2) The Timothy injunction which says "You should not rebuke an Elder, but entreat (to call near, to invite, invoke beseech to exhort entreat) him as a father and to the younger men as a brother to them" (1 Timothy 5:1) did not say they should not been spoken to or have spoken to/ confront leadership when they are in sin; It only describes both the protocol and posture one should take, i.e. leadership should speak to leadership. Please understand then that if a person knows that someone in church leadership is living a double standard life in immortality then they have the Biblical right to confront the matter by bring it to the attention of those at that level and let them deal with it, not in pride or self-righteousness, but in the fear of the lord as a brother/a member of the family of the household of faith. (1 Corinthians Chapter 5)

3) If the church leader or anyone for that matter is known to have molested or is molesting a child aged 0-16 years, whether his own or someone else's, the matter is not just a church matter but a criminal matter as well and must be reported to the police and to others in the Church leadership simultaneously, since it is not just a morality problem but a criminal act as well (Romans 13:1-5; 1 Timothy 1:9).

The Biblically Required *Response From Leadership*

Leadership must act once any case of immorality involving leadership comes before them by doing the following:

➤ **Firstly** – removing such persons from active ministry pending investigation;

➤ **Secondly** – investigating thoroughly to find truth and evidence of misconduct or behavior or habits of the particular offenses in that person life. Similar to our current laws, biblically no one is to be found guilty on the testimony of one witness (especially those in leadership). There should be at least three credible witnesses. Modern law puts it like this; 1) eyewitness report; 2) scientific or forensic evidence; and 3) circumstantial evidence.

➤ **Thirdly** - if found to be true, then this person should be removed from public ministry immediately and be subjected (them and their family) to counseling and mentorship and/or deliverance until they have proven themselves fit to be restored to leadership. The Bible does not recommend us simply moving them to another district church and putting them over an unsuspecting church. If the person fails to change they must be permanently stripped of all ministry offices and a public rebuke be done stating the reason (the sin) for such an action that the body will fear and be spared (1 Corinthians 5:1-5). "Open rebuke is better than secret love (Proverbs 27:5). The victims must be helped too.

Victim Support/Help

In the Old Testament (Deuteronomy 22) it would appear that nothing much is said about rape and abuse victims in terms of help and support.

There is more than enough said to give insight to our modern system of laws as to how it ought to conduct itself on such matters.

The 'eye for an eye, tooth for a tooth' stipulation (biblical law) given to Moses speaks to justice and not revenge; i.e. justice is not finally done until the punishment matches the crime.

The law of passivity or silence versus speaking out (Deuteronomy 22:23-27). This passage implies that a failure to expose the attack and attacker could be misconstrued or imply agreement or consent. "If she did not cry (make an alarm) then they both should be held accountable. However, if she does cry (make an alarm), whether in the city or out in the field then the man should be held accountable and the punishment matching the crime applied. Once the victim has spoken up/out then there are three tiers of leadership that' should come to her aid/defense.

1) *The spiritual leadership or authority in her home, her father*. He should be the first one to defend the cause of his daughter by fighting through the channels to get her justice, reclaim her dignity and honor and protect her name and her heritage.

2) *The spiritual leader/authority over a church, city or community (the Elder).* This leader should take the side of God to give justice to the victim and her family by ensuring that the matter is investigated, brought to trial and that even payment or punishment demanded by the law and the father or husband be carried out.

3) *Finally, the Justice leaders*. The law enforcement agencies of the nation should stand in support of the cause of God in giving justice to all in these cases (Romans 13:1-7); (1 Timothy1:8-10).

By the coming together of these three powerful tiers of leadership, the Bible said evil will be purged from the land. An example of three-tiered leadership in action was done between Judges 19:22-20:1-48. The only difference in this case was that the husband was the spiritual leader of the wife.

In the case of verbal abuse and slander of a married woman by her husband, her father must lead the charge to protect her honor, especially when she is accused of being unfaithful and her integrity and character is being questioned. (Deuteronomy 22:13-19).

Brawta

(Brawh-tah - something extra)

"Let the Redeemed of the Lord Say so" Psalm 107:2

- I am bought with price – (1 Corinthians 6:20a)
- I am forgiven - Colossians (1:13, 14)
- I am saved by grace through faith – (Ephesians 2:8)
- I am redeemed from the hand of the enemy – (Psalm 107:2)
- I am sanctified – (Corinthians 6:11)
- I am Justified – (Romans 5:1)
- I am a new creature - (2 Corinthians 5:17)
- I am child of God – (Romans 8: 16)
- I am partaker of His Divine nature – (2 Peter 1:4)
- I am redeemed from the curse or the law – (Galatians 3:13)
- I am delivered from the power of darkness – (Colossians 1:13)
- I am led by the spirit of God – (Romans 8:14)
- I am a son of God – (Romans 8:14)
- I am kept safe wherever I go – (Psalm 91:11)
- I am getting my needs met by Jesus – (Philippians 4:19)
- I am casting all my cares of Jesus – (1Peter 5:7)
- I am strong in the Lord and in His mighty power – (Ephesians 6:10)
- I am filled with the Spirit of wisdom, power and the fear of the Lord – (Micah 3:8)
- I am doing all things through Christ who strengthens me – (Philippians 4:13)

- I am an heir of God and joint heir with Jesus – (Romans 8:17)
- I am heir to the blessing of Abraham – (Galatians 3:13,14)
- I am observing and doing the Lord's commandments – (Deuteronomy 28:12)
- I am blessed coming in and going out – (Deuteronomy 28:6)
- I am an inheritor coming in and going out – (1John 5:11, 12)
- I am blessed with all spiritual blessings – (Ephesians 1:3)
- I am healed by His stripes – (1Peter 2:24)
- I am exercising my authority over the enemy – (Luke 10:19)
- I am above only and not beneath – (Deuteronomy 28:13)
- I am more than a conqueror – (Romans 8:37)
- I am establishing God's Word here on earth – (Matthew 16:19)
- I am forcefully advancing the kingdom of Christ – (Matthew 10:7,)
- I am an over comer by Jesus' Blood and my testimony – (Revelation 12:11)
- I am daily overcoming the devil – (1 John 4; 4)
- I am not moved by what I see – (2 Corinthians 4:18)
- I am walking by faith and not by sight – (2 Corinthians 5:7)
- I am casting down vain imagination – (2 Corinthians10:18)
- I am waging war with mighty weapons – (2 Corinthians 10: 4)
- I am bringing every thought into captivity – (2 Corinthians 10:5)
- I am being transformed by the renewing of my mind – (Romans 12:1, 2)
- I am renewing in the spirit / attitude of my mind – (Ephesians 4:23)
- I am a co-labourer with God – (1Corithians 3:9)
- I am the righteousness of God in Christ – (2 Corinthians 5:21)
- I am an imitator of Jesus – (Ephesians 5:1)
- I am the light of the world – (Matthew 5:14)

About the Author

Rev. Wayne E. A. Palmer

Reverend Wayne Palmer has been walking with the Lord Jesus for the past 32 years and is a living testimony of the powerful grace of God. Saved from a life of revivalism, he now witnesses boldly for the Lord wherever the Spirit of the Lord leads. Reverend Palmer has been entrusted with the Apostolic and Prophetic mantles as he teaches the Body of Christ and equips the Saints from another level of Kingdom living. He has ministered extensively across Jamaica and has done ministry in the Cayman Islands, the United States of America and the Eastern Caribbean as Psalmist, and Conference Speaker. His areas of specialization include Praise and Worship, Deliverance and Spiritual Warfare, Marriage Counseling and Leadership Training, Church Stewardship, Occultism and Cultism, and many other areas that are relevant to the advancement and edification of the Kingdom of God.

He yearns for the unity and the maturity of God's people, preparing them for an end-time revival and the coming of our Lord and Savior Jesus the Christ. He is presently the Senior Pastor of Jubilee Worship Centre located in Spanish Town, St. Catherine. He gives oversight to four registered independent churches in Jamaica and acts as mentor to many others. He also serves as a guest lecturer. Reverend Palmer is the happy husband of Melody for twenty-two years and from their union has fathered their two sons, Stephen and Israel. He holds a Diploma in Biblical studies from the Jamaica Open Bible Institute (JOBI) now College of Theological and Interdisciplinary Studies (CTICS), and a Bachelor of Theology, from Cornerstone University USA.

Contact Information:

Email: rev11.15@live.com ; jamaicaspsalmist@gmail.com
Telephone: 1(876)771-3445

www.ingramcontent.com/pod-product-compliance
Lightning Source LLC
Chambersburg PA
CBHW062001040426
42447CB00010B/1858